Among the titles in this series

EDITED AND INTRODUCED BY MARY-ALICE WATERS

It's the Poor Who Face the Savagery of the US 'Justice' System
THE CUBAN FIVE TALK ABOUT THEIR LIVES
WITHIN THE US WORKING CLASS (2016)

Absolved by Solidarity/Absuelto por la solidaridad
BY ANTONIO GUERRERO (2015)

Voices from Prison: The Cuban Five
BY RAFAEL CANCEL MIRANDA, GERARDO HERNÁNDEZ,
RAMÓN LABAÑINO, AND OTHERS (2014)

Cuba and Angola: Fighting for Africa's Freedom and Our Own
BY FIDEL CASTRO, RAÚL CASTRO, NELSON MANDELA, AND OTHERS (2013)

Women in Cuba: The Making of a Revolution Within the Revolution
BY VILMA ESPÍN, ASELA DE LOS SANTOS, AND YOLANDA FERRER (2012)

The First and Second Declarations of Havana
(2007)

Our History Is Still Being Written
BY ARMANDO CHOY, GUSTAVO CHUI, AND MOISÉS SÍO WONG (2005)

Marianas in Combat
BY TETÉ PUEBLA (2003)

From the Escambray to the Congo
BY VÍCTOR DREKE (2002)

Playa Girón/Bay of Pigs
BY FIDEL CASTRO AND JOSÉ RAMÓN FERNÁNDEZ (2001)

Cuba and the Coming American Revolution
BY JACK BARNES (2001)

Che Guevara Talks to Young People
(2000)

Making History
INTERVIEWS WITH FOUR CUBAN GENERALS (1999)

Pombo: A Man of Che's *guerrilla*
BY HARRY VILLEGAS (1997)

How Far We Slaves Have Come!
BY NELSON MANDELA AND FIDEL CASTRO (1991)

CUBA & ANGOLA THE WAR FOR FREEDOM

CUBA & ANGOLA
THE WAR FOR FREEDOM

HARRY VILLEGAS
"POMBO"

Pathfinder
NEW YORK LONDON MONTREAL SYDNEY

Edited by Martín Koppel and Mary-Alice Waters

ISBN 978-1-60488-093-9
Library of Congress Control Number 2016961455
Manufactured in the United States of America

COVER DESIGN: Toni Gorton
COVER PHOTO: Cuban helicopter on support mission during battle of Cangamba, Angola, August 1983. (Verde Olivo)
PHOTO PAGES: Carole Caron

Pathfinder
www.pathfinderpress.com
E-mail: pathfinder@pathfinderpress.com

Contents

Maps

Photos

Abbreviations

FAPLA	People's Armed Forces for the Liberation of Angola (*Forças Armadas Populares de Libertação de Angola*)
FAR	Revolutionary Armed Forces of Cuba (*Fuerzas Armadas Revolucionarias*)
FNLA	National Front for the Liberation of Angola (*Frente Nacional de a Libertação de Angola*)
FRELIMO	Mozambique Liberation Front (*Frente de Libertação de Moçambique*)
MPLA	Popular Movement for the Liberation of Angola (*Movimento Popular de Libertação de Angola*)
PAIGC	African Party for the Independence of Guinea and Cape Verde (*Partido Africano da Independência da Guiné e Cabo Verde*)
RENAMO	Mozambican National Resistance (*Resistência Nacional Moçambicana*)
SWAPO	South West Africa People's Organisation
UNITA	National Union for the Total Independence of Angola (*União Nacional para a Independência Total de Angola*)

COURTESY HARRY VILLEGAS

MARTÍN KOPPEL/MILITANT

Top: Harry Villegas, "Pombo" (center, sitting), in Negage, Angola, when he headed Cuban regiment in Angola's northern region, late 1970s.

Bottom: During interview in Havana at national offices of Association of Combatants of the Cuban Revolution, November 2009.

About the author

Harry Villegas was born in 1940 in the village of Yara, in the foothills of the Sierra Maestra mountains in eastern Cuba. As a teenager he joined the struggle against the US-backed dictatorship of Fulgencio Batista, taking part in clandestine activities in the city of Manzanillo.

In 1957 Villegas joined the Rebel Army, where he served in Column 4 under the command of Ernesto Che Guevara. Villegas took part in numerous combat actions and fought in the column led by Guevara that crossed Cuba to open a new front in the Escambray mountains. In December 1958 he took part in the battle of Santa Clara, the last major battle of the revolutionary war.

After the fall of the Batista dictatorship on January 1, 1959, Villegas served as head of Guevara's escort. In 1960–1961 the revolutionary government supported massive working-class mobilizations that expropriated Cuba's industries and placed them under state ownership. Working alongside Guevara, who became minister of industry, Villegas took on responsibilities as a factory manager, helping to lead working people to restructure industrial production and place it on new foundations. He returned to active military duty the following year.

In 1965 Villegas volunteered for an internationalist mission in Africa. He served on the general staff of a column of more than a hundred Cubans, led by Guevara, fighting alongside anti-imperialist forces in the Congo. During this campaign Villegas received the nom de guerre he has used ever since: Pombo.

Around the world he is best known as one of the Cuban revolutionaries who fought alongside Guevara in Bolivia in 1966–67, where he also served on the general staff. The aim of the campaign was to open a revolutionary struggle for power in the countries of Latin America's Southern Cone. Guevara fell in combat in October 1967, and Villegas commanded the five surviving Cuban and Bolivian guerrillas who eluded encirclement by the Bolivian army and US intelligence forces. He and the two other Cubans escaped across the border into Chile and arrived in Havana in March 1968. His account of this campaign, *Pombo: A Man of Che's 'guerrilla,'* is published by Editora Política (Spanish), Pathfinder (English), and Éditions Graphein (French).

For most of the 1970s Villegas commanded the Border Brigade in Guantánamo. That unit of the Revolutionary Armed Forces (FAR) protects Cuba at its border with the US naval base at Guantánamo Bay, the Cuban territory occupied by Washington for more than a century against the will of the Cuban people.

In 1977–79, Villegas helped lead Cuba's volunteer military mission in Angola, defending the newly independent country against the apartheid regime of South Africa and its backers in Washington and other imperialist powers. He commanded the Motorized Infantry Regiment in the northern region, a Cuban unit that collaborated with the Angolan army. Returning to Cuba in 1979, he commanded the motorized infantry regiment of the FAR's Tank Division.

In 1981, he was assigned as liaison between the Cuban high command in Angola and the Revolutionary Armed Forces special command post in Havana, headed by Fidel Castro. After the decisive defeat of the South African forces in 1988 at the battle of Cuito Cuanavale, Villegas remained in Angola. As head of operations for the Cuban mission, he helped plan the withdrawal of Cuban forces.

After returning to Cuba in 1990, Villegas led the Political Section of Cuba's Western Army, and served as a member of the Operations Directorate of the General Staff of the Revolutionary Armed Forces. He was a member of the Central Committee of the Communist Party of Cuba from 1997 to 2011, a deputy to the National Assembly of People's Power, and served as executive vice president of the Association of Combatants of the Cuban Revolution. He also served as military adviser to the attorney general's office. Retired from active duty, he holds the rank of brigadier general.

Villegas has received more than fifty decorations, including four awards for valor. In 1995 he was named Hero of the Republic of Cuba, the highest honor given by Cuba's Council of State.

Introduction

MARY-ALICE WATERS

Those unwilling to fight for the freedom of others will never be able to fight for their own.

FIDEL CASTRO
Pinar del Río, July 1976

If our people know themselves better, if all of us know much better what we are capable of achieving, that too is thanks to Angola!

RAUL CASTRO
Havana, May 1991

BETWEEN 1975 AND 1991, some 425,000 Cuban volunteers, organized by Cuba's revolutionary leadership, served in Angola. In various deployments, they went there in response to a call for assistance from the Angolan government. In 1975 the people of that African country had just wrested freedom from Portugal after nearly five centuries of brutal colonial exploitation and domination. Now they were under attack by the white-supremacist regime of South Africa and its African and international allies.

The purpose of the Cuban mission, which stretched over sixteen years, was to help Angola defend itself and decisively repel this military aggression backed by Washington. The mission ended only after the armed forces of the apartheid regime had been dealt a decisive defeat in March 1988 at the battle of Cuito Cuanavale in southern Angola while, at the same time, a formidable force of Cuban, Angolan, and Namibian combatants swept south, toward the bases of the South African regime in its colony, Namibia.

Simultaneously fearful of the exploding mass antiapartheid struggle within South Africa itself, Pretoria sued for peace. A tripartite agreement between Angola, South Africa, and Cuba, negotiated over five months, was signed at United Nations headquarters in New York in December 1988. It recognized not only the legitimacy and sovereignty of the Angolan government in Luanda but also the independence of Namibia. It gave further confidence to workers and youth in South Africa fighting the apartheid state.

As Nelson Mandela, the central leader of the struggle to bring down the racist regime, told the people of Cuba and the world in July 1991, the defeat of the South African army at Cuito Cuanavale was made possible by Cuba's "unparalleled" contribution. It was "a victory for all of Africa," he said, "a turning point in the struggle to free the continent and our country from the scourge of apartheid!"

Cuba and Angola: The War for Freedom is a first-hand account of that historic internationalist mission in Angola, as told by Harry Villegas, a brigadier general of Cuba's Revolutionary Armed Forces (FAR), who is better known around the world as "Pombo." That was the Swahili nom de guerre given to Villegas by Ernesto Che Guevara. Pombo fought at Che's side for a decade—first in the revolutionary war on Cuban soil that brought down the US-backed dictatorship of Fulgencio Batista in January 1959, and then in internationalist missions in the Congo and Bolivia.

After Guevara fell in battle in Bolivia in October 1967, Villegas led the five surviving combatants of Che's guerrilla front—two Bolivians and three Cubans—who evaded capture by the Bolivian army and US intelligence forces for four months. Villegas and the two other Cubans eventually escaped across the border into Chile, and in March 1968 they returned to Havana.

■

In April 1974 the fifty-year-old, deeply decayed fascist dictatorship in Portugal was overthrown in a military coup led by young officers. A revolutionary upsurge of Portuguese workers and farmers erupted. The old regime had faced rising opposition at home, as well as advancing national liberation struggles in each of its African colonies, especially Guinea-Bissau. The new government in Lisbon was forced to recognize the independence of all its African territories.

As Portugal's brutal colonial hold over its African empire was being broken, other imperialist powers had for years been maneuvering to grab what they could. With independence day for Angola—Portugal's largest and richest colony—approaching on November 11, 1975, they accelerated their efforts.

Just months earlier, in April 1975, the victorious national liberation forces of Vietnam had driven US troops and personnel out of Saigon, soon renamed Ho Chi Minh City. Now, on top of that blow to the imperialist world order, the future of all southern Africa was at stake, from the Congo and what was then Rhodesia (now Zimbabwe), down to the Cape of Good Hope. For Pretoria—encouraged and backhandedly supplied by Washington—survival of the apartheid regime itself was on the table.

The first invasion of Angola by South African and Zairean troops began in October 1975 as armored columns crossed the border from their bases in South-West Africa (Namibia) and drove north. A military offensive simultaneously swept south from Zaire (Congo). Zaire's proimperialist Mobutu dictatorship hoped to annex the oil-rich province of Cabinda and take whatever other Angolan territory it could.

The objective of these combined operations was to conquer Luanda, the capital city, before November 11, to prevent the installation of a government headed by the Popular Movement for the Liberation of Angola (MPLA), the strongest of the anticolonial movements, with the broadest popular base. With planned celebrations barely a week away, Luanda was in danger of falling.

The response of the leadership of the Cuban government and people to the urgent request for aid from Angola's MPLA-led provisional government was immediate and decisive. Within hours Operation Carlota was launched—named in tribute to the African woman who had led two rebellions against slavery and colonial oppression in Cuba before being captured and brutally executed in 1843.

The day before the independence ceremony in Luanda, some 200 just-landed Cuban internationalist volunteers joined the Angolan defenders. Together they turned back the column moving south from Zaire that was poised on the doorsteps of the capital. The immediate objective of South Africa and its imperialist allies had been stymied.

Less than five months later, with thirty-six thousand Cuban volunteers by then on the ground, allied with Angolan troops, the military forces of both the South African apartheid regime and Mobutu dictatorship had been driven out of Angola.

But that was only the beginning.

More than a decade of what was euphemistically called "low intensity warfare" against the Angolan regime ensued. South African forces regularly operated deep in Angolan territory in support of UNITA, Pretoria's Angolan ally, led by Jonas Savimbi. The brutality of the war was enormous, with Angolan casualties eventually rising to hundreds of thousands. Nearly 2,100 Cubans also lost their lives on Angolan soil before their mission was completed.

Then, in late 1987, South African troops began their second major invasion in hopes of inflicting a crushing defeat on Angolan forces. But the apartheid regime had once again miscalculated—the crushing defeat was theirs.

The Cuban and Angolan leaderships had come to agreement, as Cuban leader Fidel Castro put it, that the time was ripe to "cut off the hands" of South Africa in Angola, and that is what they did. The March 1988 victory at a village in southern Angola known as Cuito Cuanavale echoed around the world—and across South Africa above all. In Nelson Mandela's words, that victory "broke the myth of the invincibility of the white oppressors."

Less than two years later, Mandela, imprisoned for more than twenty-seven years by the apartheid state, walked free. By 1994 the racist regime was no more, and Mandela was president of South Africa.

■

In May 1991 Cuban Minister of the Revolutionary Armed Forces Raúl Castro welcomed home the last unit of internationalist volunteers returning from Angola. "When we face new and unexpected challenges," he told the Cuban people, "we will always be able to recall the epic of Angola with gratitude, because without Angola we would not be as strong as we are today."

The truth of those words was soon put to the test. As the Soviet Union and its allied regimes in Eastern and Central Europe shattered between 1989 and 1991, some 85 percent of Cuba's foreign trade disappeared, almost overnight, crippling agricultural and industrial production, transportation, electrical generation, and much more. The Cuban Revolution confronted the most severe economic, and political, crisis in its history. Enemies of the revolution around the world started packing their bags in anticipation of what they believed would be a triumphal return to Havana.

Instead, it was the creativity and steadfastness of Cuba's working people that triumphed, as they organized against all odds to produce and to defend their socialist revolution. One element underpinning that victory was the proletarian confidence gained over the years of the Angolan mission—and, in the late 1980s, the simultaneous rebirth in Cuba of a mass social movement of volunteer labor to build housing, schools, clinics, child care centers, and other social necessities.

The hundreds of thousands of Cubans who over the years had taken part in the epic feat in Africa returned knowing much better the true face of capitalist exploitation and imperialist domination. And in Raúl's words, Cuban working people knew "much better what we are capable of achieving."

The political education and combat leadership experience gained by new generations of Cubans during the Angola mission was nowhere better revealed than in the example set by the Cuban revolutionaries who became known around the world as the Cuban Five.

Arrested in Florida in 1998, where they were monitoring the activities of Cuban counterrevolutionary organizations planning attacks on Cuban and US targets, the five were railroaded to prison by the Clinton administration on fabricated charges that included conspiracy to commit espionage and even murder. They each served draconian sentences of up to sixteen years behind bars. Their freedom and return home to Cuba, including the release of the final three on December 17, 2014, was won only through their own steadfastness and the relentless work of the Cuban government together with a hard-fought international solidarity campaign.

Three of the five—Gerardo Hernández, Fernando González, and René González—had served in Angola. Their stories told firsthand can be found in Pathfinder's *Cuba and Angola: Fighting for Africa's Freedom and Our Own.* For each of them, as they have explained many times over, their time as part of this internationalist military mission was an experience that transformed their lives and on which they drew continuously for strength throughout their long years of incarceration.

■

Cuba and Angola: The War for Freedom by Harry Villegas is not a military memoir. It does contain powerful eyewitness accounts of moments of combat and decisive battles in Cangamba and Cuito Cuanavale among others. Its greatest value, however, lies in the political lessons it conveys—lessons, as Pombo makes clear, that were impressed on him above all by Commander in Chief Fidel Castro, with whom he worked on this mission for more than half a decade.

General Harry Villegas served three tours of duty in Angola, one from 1977 to 1979 at the head of the Motorized Infantry Regiment in the northern region. The Cuban unit collaborated with the Angolan army in mop-up operations against the Zairian-backed forces of Holden Roberto's FNLA.

From 1981 to 1988 Villegas served as liaison between the Cuban command headquarters in Angola and the special command post in Cuba of the Revolutionary Armed Forces, headed by Fidel Castro. In that capacity, as Pombo describes in these pages, he was the eyes and ears of the central command in Havana. He traveled constantly between the two countries, responsible for keeping the general staff in Havana objectively and accurately informed of all important developments in Angola and conveying precise instructions back to the head of the mission on the battlefront.

After the accords were signed in December 1988, Villegas remained in Angola as head of operations for the Cuban mission, helping to plan the withdrawal of the Cuban forces. On returning to Cuba in 1990, he led the Political Section of Cuba's Western Army, and served as a member of the Operations Directorate of the General Staff of the Revolutionary Armed Forces until his retirement from active duty.

It is on this experience that Villegas bases his rich account, aimed first and foremost at the political education of new generations of revolutionary combatants.

■

Cuba and Angola: The War for Freedom is the product of multiple interviews with Harry Villegas between 2009 and 2016. Each round amplified and clarified details of previous discussions. In addition, during those years dozens of memoirs of the Angola mission appeared in Cuba, published by Verde Olivo, Editora Política, and others.

Firsthand accounts by those who served in Angola include books by General Ramón Espinosa, vice minister of the FAR; General Raúl Tomassevich, who twice headed the military mission in Angola; his adjutant Lt. Colonel José Gárciga; and Lt. Colonel Jorge Martín Blandino. These and other accounts too numerous to mention proved indispensable for understanding political and military events and verifying names, dates, and other facts.

Published in the US in 2013, and in Cuba in 2015, *Visions of Freedom: Havana, Washington, Pretoria, and the Struggle for*

Southern Africa, 1976–1991 by Piero Gleijeses, became an additional source of valuable information.

The Pathfinder editors who interviewed Pombo and worked with him to bring his account to completion—Martín Koppel, Róger Calero, and I—are grateful for the generous help we received from so many, starting with Pombo himself. Special appreciation is also owed Iraida Aguirrechu and José Gárciga for their editorial assistance throughout, as well as to Verde Olivo publishing house, Casa Editora Abril and *Granma* newspaper for making available many of the photos that appear in this book.

It is to revolutionary combatants of the present and future that *Cuba and Angola: The War for Freedom* is addressed. We are confident it will serve them well in the battles ahead.

December 2016

Africa

Morocco
Tunisia
Algeria
Libya
Egypt
Western Sahara
Cape Verde
Mauritania
Mali
Niger
Chad
Eritrea
Gambia
Senegal
Guinea-Bissau
Burkina Faso
Sudan
Djibouti
Guinea (Conakry)
Benin
Sierra Leone
Côte d'Ivoire
Ghana
Nigeria
Ethiopia
Liberia
Central African Republic
Somalia
Togo
Cameroon
Equatorial Guinea
Uganda
Kenya
EQUATOR
São Tomé & Príncipe
Gabon
Democratic Republic of Congo (Zaire)
Rwanda
Burundi
Tanzania
Republic of Congo (Brazzaville)
Angola
Mozambique
Zambia
Malawi
Madagascar
Atlantic Ocean
Zimbabwe
Namibia
Botswana
0
500 miles
0
1000 kilometers
Swaziland
South Africa
Lesotho
N
W
E
S

Angola provinces

Angola

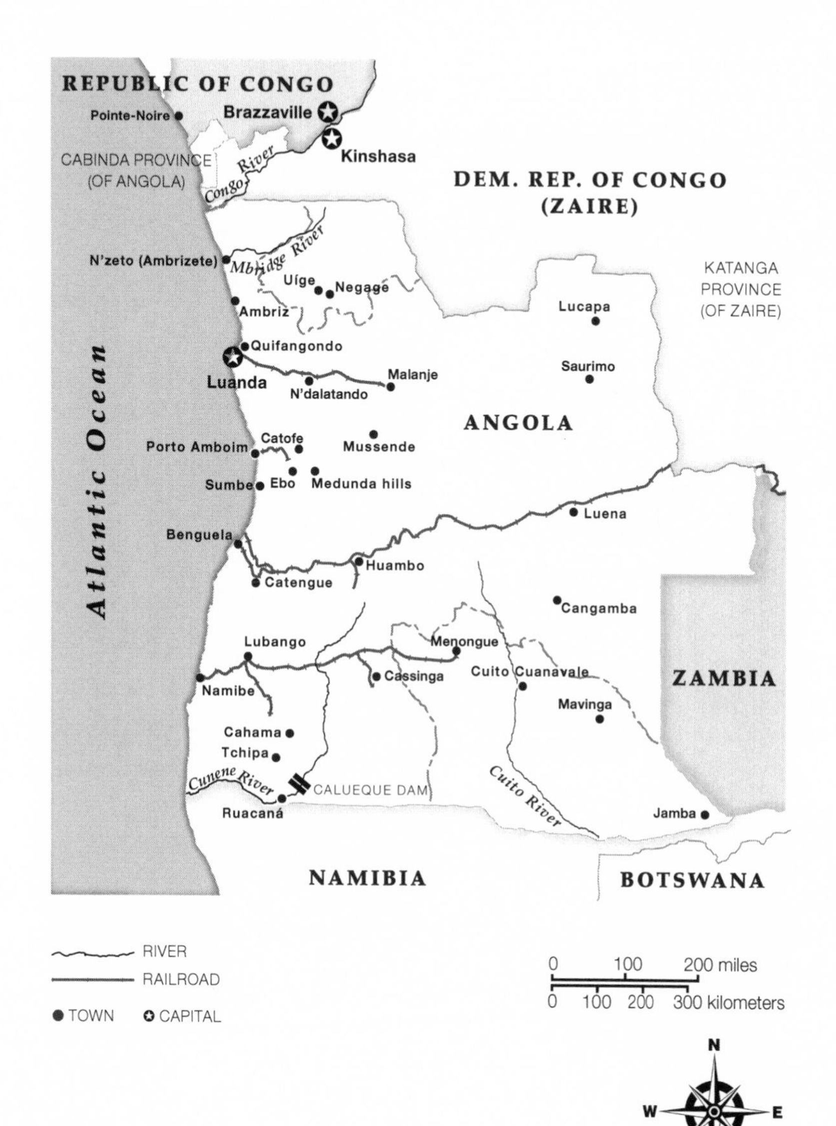

REPUBLIC OF CONGO
Pointe-Noire
Brazzaville
Kinshasa
CABINDA PROVINCE
(OF ANGOLA)
Congo River
DEM. REP. OF CONGO
(ZAIRE)
N'zeto (Ambrizete)
Mbridge River
Uíge
Negage
Ambriz
KATANGA
PROVINCE
(OF ZAIRE)
Lucapa
Quifangondo
Luanda
N'dalatando
Malanje
Saurimo
ANGOLA
Atlantic Ocean
Porto Amboim
Catofe
Mussende
Sumbe
Ebo
Medunda hills
Luena
Benguela
Huambo
Catengue
Cangamba
Lubango
Menongue
Namibe
Cassinga
Cuito Cuanavale
ZAMBIA
Mavinga
Cahama
Tchipa
Cunene River
CALUEQUE DAM
Ruacaná
Cuito River
Jamba
NAMIBIA
BOTSWANA
RIVER
RAILROAD
TOWN
CAPITAL
0 100 200 miles
0 100 200 300 kilometers
N
W
E
S

Our internationalism in Africa was born with the Cuban Revolution

MARY-ALICE WATERS: At a mass rally in the city of Matanzas, Cuba, on July 26, 1991, Nelson Mandela, leader of the South African freedom struggle, paid tribute to the Cuban people. Mandela had been released from prison only a year earlier, after some twenty-seven years behind the bars of the white-supremacist apartheid regime.

Let me begin by reading a few paragraphs of what Mandela said to the tens of thousands of Cubans assembled in Matanzas, and to the world:

> It was in prison when I first heard of the massive assistance that the Cuban internationalist forces provided the people of Angola, on such a scale that one hesitated to believe, when the Angolans came under combined attack of South Africa, CIA-financed FNLA, mercenary, UNITA, and Zairean troops in 1975.
>
> We in Africa are used to being victims of countries wanting to carve up our territory and subvert our sovereignty. It is unparalleled in African history to have another people rise to the defense of one of us.
>
> We know also that this was a popular action in Cuba. We are aware that those who fought and died in Angola were only a small proportion of those who volunteered.

> For the Cuban people, internationalism is not merely a word but something we have seen practiced to the benefit of large sections of humankind.

Pombo, you were one of the Cubans who led that unparalleled action spanning sixteen years, from 1975 to 1991. During those years, more than four hundred thousand Cuban men and women went to Angola as internationalist volunteers. They not only helped the Angolan people defend their independence against invading forces of the white supremacist regime. They helped the people of Namibia win their independence from South Africa. And their actions added to the massive revolutionary upsurge of the South African people that put an end to the apartheid regime.

In short, as Nelson Mandela declared in Matanzas in 1991, these victories made possible by Cuban solidarity changed the course of history in Africa and the world. Today, however, this history is little known among working people and youth in the United States. It is little known among several generations of youth in Africa, and even here in Cuba the memory is fading.

How did Cuba's participation in Angola's liberation struggle begin?

HARRY VILLEGAS: We have to place the Cuban mission in Angola within a broader framework. As Fidel has said, for us internationalism is paying our debt to humanity. Many of us in Cuba are of African descent. Thousands of Africans and their descendants participated in our struggles against slavery and for independence.

Cuban internationalism in Africa begins with the first years of the Cuban Revolution. It begins in Algeria. In 1961, when the Algerian people were fighting for independence from France, Cuba sent them a shipload of weapons.

Independence was won in 1962. The first thing we did was

To be internationalists is to pay our debt to humanity

We know the United States had some sleepless nights over the boldness with which a small country like Cuba has carried out an internationalist mission of this nature [to aid Angola]. That a small Caribbean country was capable of providing support to a sister African nation is something beyond their conception.

We know what the people of Africa think—and this is another weighty problem for US policy. The people of Africa see the United States as an ally of apartheid, responsible for its survival.

Cuba has no economic interest in Angola or in Africa. Cuba is in Angola because we are fulfilling our duty to help other peoples.

As we have said before, to be internationalists is to pay our debt to humanity. Those who are incapable of fighting for others will never be capable of fighting for themselves.

FIDEL CASTRO
DECEMBER 5, 1988

to send volunteer doctors and other medical personnel. That was in 1963.

Later that same year, when the Moroccan regime, backed by the US, attacked Algeria, we sent soldiers and military equipment to defend the newly independent government. We didn't have to fight there; our strategy was deterrence. When the Moroccans saw we were in Algeria, they pulled out. Later, when we withdrew our troops, we left our tanks with the Algerians for their defense.

Mission in Congo, 1965

WATERS: Ten years before Cuba's internationalist mission in Angola, revolutionary leader Ernesto Che Guevara led a column of 128 Cuban combatants to the eastern Congo to help independence forces fighting the pro-imperialist regime in that country.[1] You were one of them, and served on the general staff.

VILLEGAS: In early 1965 while on a tour of several African countries Che visited Dar es Salaam, Tanzania. There he met with leaders of the Congolese revolutionary movement. It was agreed that Cuba would send instructors to support that movement. Che led the column, which fought alongside those forces for several months, from April to November 1965.

A few weeks earlier Che had visited Congo-Brazzaville, where he met with Agostinho Neto and other leaders of the MPLA (Popular Movement for the Liberation of Angola). Angola was still a Portuguese colony at the time. They reached agreement that Cuba would give military training to MPLA cadres in their independence struggle.

A column of Cuban combatants was sent to Congo-Brazzaville in 1965. It was led by Jorge Risquet; the military commander was Rolando Kindelán. That unit helped defend the government of Congo-Brazzaville, which was threatened by the pro-imperialist regime in the Congo of Mobutu Sese Seko. It also trained the guerrilla fighters who subsequently became the People's Armed Forces for the Liberation of Angola (FAPLA).

1. Two neighboring countries historically share the name Congo. *Congo-Brazzaville* (formally, Republic of Congo), won independence from France in 1960. *The Congo* (known as Zaire from 1971 to 1997, now Democratic Republic of the Congo) won independence from Belgium in 1960.

A training center was created in Congo-Brazzaville. Rafael Moracén headed the group of Cuban instructors. They trained two units of Angolans that would enter Angola to reinforce the MPLA.

The first unit, the Camilo Cienfuegos Column, was a big help to the MPLA fighters in northern Angola. The second group was captured and most were killed by the FNLA (National Liberation Front of Angola), an imperialist-backed Angolan group. Among the MPLA fighters killed was Deolinda Rodrigues, who was also a founding leader of the Organization of Angolan Women.

RÓGER CALERO: How do you assess the experience of Che's column in the Congo?

VILLEGAS: The Congo was a tremendous experience for all of us. We went there in April 1965 not to lead the war but to train and advise Congolese combatants in the liberated zones in the eastern part of the country. Fighting alongside them, we took part in ambushes and several important battles.

It was a complex situation, however. The Congolese leaders weren't there with their troops; they were living in other countries. In the end, they decided to end combat operations. We left in November 1965.

WATERS: In his book *Episodes of the Revolutionary War: Congo*,[2] Che explains that before arriving there, he and the rest of the Cuban leadership knew very little about the economic and social conditions of the Congo. He says, for example, that they weren't aware that in much of central Africa land was not private property. Unlike Cuba and the rest of Latin America, peasants fighting for land to cultivate weren't a driving force of the class struggle.

2. Ernesto Che Guevara, *The African Dream: The Diaries of the Revolutionary War in the Congo* (New York: Grove Press, 2000).

VILLEGAS: Yes, as Che pointed out in his diary, there was no concept of land ownership in the Congo. The mode of production and relations among families were different from Cuba and elsewhere in Latin America. Tribalism existed. A big part of the population looked to their tribe, and to the divisions colonialism had created, rather than to a nation. All these things have to be looked at concretely. There's no single script for the whole world and for all moments in history.

Che concluded that the economic, social, and political conditions didn't yet exist in that part of Africa to carry out a revolutionary struggle against imperialism—and might not for another twenty years.

In fact, a little more than two decades after Che made the commitment to help the MPLA, a historic victory was won when the invading South African army was defeated at Cuito Cuanavale in 1988, securing Angola's independence. So, when Cuba responded to Neto's request in 1975 to send Cuban combatants to Angola, we already had a ten-year history of working with the MPLA. We had already been in Angola helping their independence struggle.

MARTÍN KOPPEL: After the Cuban missions in the Congo and Congo-Brazzaville, in 1966 Cuban internationalists joined combatants in Guinea-Bissau in their struggle for independence from Portuguese colonialism.

VILLEGAS: Yes, Cuba helped with instructors and combatants until Guinea-Bissau won its independence in 1974. This support was very important. I can't tell you much in detail about this since I wasn't in Guinea-Bissau. Víctor Dreke was head of the Cuban military mission there and he talks about it in his book, *From the Escambray to the Congo: In the Whirlwind of the Cuban Revolution.*[3]

3. Published by Pathfinder in 2002.

Fidel and Che had a very high opinion of the leadership of the Guinea-Bissau liberation movement, of the outstanding qualities of Amilcar Cabral as a revolutionary and leader. The party led by Cabral, the PAIGC (African Party for the Independence of Guinea and Cape Verde), was a well-defined, disciplined movement. They benefited from the strong support of Ahmed Sékou Touré, president of neighboring Guinea-Conakry, which the PAIGC was able to use as a base of operations.

Fall of Portuguese empire and defeat of South Africa's first invasion, 1975–76

WATERS: What was the relationship between the advancing independence struggle in Guinea-Bissau and Cape Verde and the collapse of the decayed fascist dictatorship in Portugal in 1974? How did the victory in Guinea-Bissau affect the liberation struggles in Portugal's other major African colonies, Mozambique and Angola?

VILLEGAS: The war in Guinea-Bissau was a turning point in the anticolonial struggle.

The Portuguese government's defeat by the Guinean people was the detonator of Portugal's so-called Carnation Revolution. The growing casualties the Portuguese were suffering in Guinea-Bissau and the economic and moral price of the conflict convinced the high command of the armed forces they couldn't win the war. They had to get rid of the main obstacle to resolving this problem: the fifty-year-old fascist dictatorship. They deposed the dictator, Marcelo Caetano, in a coup. That opened the door to the popular upsurge.

The new government ceded independence to all Portugal's African colonies—Guinea-Bissau, Cape Verde, São Tomé and Príncipe, Mozambique, and Angola. They had been under Portuguese rule for five hundred years. The government signed agreements to hand over power to the strongest organization in each country. In Guinea-Bissau that was the

PAIGC. In Mozambique it was FRELIMO (Mozambique Liberation Front).

But in Angola there were three contending organizations. The MPLA, whose central leader was Agostinho Neto, had a long history of fighting the Portuguese. It was the organization that enjoyed the widest support among the population.

The FNLA (National Front for the Liberation of Angola) and UNITA (National Union for the Total Independence of Angola) were pro-imperialist organizations. Both received CIA aid. The FNLA, whose leader was Holden Roberto, was backed by the Mobutu dictatorship in Zaire with troops and equipment. UNITA, headed by Jonas Savimbi, had the support of the racist regime of South Africa.

Each of the three Angolan organizations had a different ethnic base. The FNLA had influence among the Bakongo people in northeast Angola. The MPLA's greatest strength was among the Mbundu, the majority ethnic group in the north-central region. UNITA had its base further south, among the Ovimbundu.

Neto and other MPLA leaders thought less in narrow racial terms than the other two groups. The MPLA included members who were *mestiço* (of mixed African and Portuguese descent) and tried to move beyond tribal divisions.

In early 1975 the Portuguese signed an agreement with the MPLA, FNLA, and UNITA—the Alvor Agreement—to grant independence to Angola on November 11 of that year. A coalition government was established with representatives of all three groups.

But armed conflict soon broke out between the three organizations. Each strove to gain control of the capital city of Luanda by the day Portugal handed over power.

The MPLA had a strong base of support in Luanda. The FNLA began to move its troops from Zaire and northern Angola toward the capital. UNITA's base was in Huambo, in the south-central region of the country. The South African military began training UNITA and FNLA troops in southern Angola.

How Angola mission began

CALERO: How did the Cuban military mission in Angola begin?

VILLEGAS: Neto had asked Cuba for military instructors to train the FAPLA (People's Armed Forces for the Liberation of Angola) and transform the guerrilla force into a national army. In August 1975, a Cuban delegation headed by Commander Raúl Díaz Argüelles went to Angola to make preparations.

The first Cubans to arrive were instructors. Only after the South African invasion in October were Cuban combat troops sent to Angola.

The FAPLA leadership proposed that the Cuban instructors be dispersed with a small group in each province. Fidel had a different approach, which turned out to be well-founded. He proposed setting up training centers with at least seventy Cuban combatants in each—that is, units with sufficient combat capacity to fight on their own if attacked.

The Angolans accepted Fidel's proposal and four Centers for Revolutionary Instruction were established. They were located in Cabinda, Saurimo, N'dalatando, and Benguela. In all there were nearly five hundred instructors, many more than the hundred Neto had requested.

Almost half the instructors were in Cabinda. Why there? Because Angola's economy was based on income from oil extracted in Cabinda, and still is. We needed to maintain a strong presence there, Fidel pointed out, since there would be offensives from Zaire and we'd have to face more complex conditions than elsewhere in the country. Cabinda is separated from the rest of Angola by a narrow strip of Zairean

We called this mission *Operation Carlota*

"In Cuba we gave this internationalist mission the name 'Carlota' in homage to an exceptional African woman who, as a slave on Cuban soil, led two rebellions against colonial oppression and who —just as they wanted to do to Angola in 1975—was dismembered by the butchers who succeeded in capturing her during the second uprising."

—Raúl Castro
May 27, 1991

On November 5, 1843, Carlota, a slave on the Triunvirato sugar mill near Matanzas, Cuba, led a slave rebellion. It was crushed by Spanish colonial troops, and Carlota was drawn and quartered.

territory that extends to the Atlantic coast.

Planes carrying the instructors left Cuba in early October. Weapons and ammunition were sent by ship. They unloaded at Pointe-Noire, Congo-Brazzaville, and near Porto Amboim, on the coast of central Angola.

On October 14, 1975, the South Africans—backed by the US government—invaded Angola from the south, crossing the Namibian border. Accompanied by UNITA troops, they rapidly moved north, approaching Luanda.

When the invaders reached Catengue, near the training center in Benguela, the FAPLA troops and Cuban instructors there put up resistance. But they couldn't contain the advance of the South Africans, who had the advantage both in numbers and in weapons. The Angolan and Cuban forces had to retreat. Four Cuban instructors died there—our first casualties in Angola.

It was then that the Angolan government requested that Cuba send combat troops to help them defeat the aggression. Our leadership met the request. On November 5, 1975, Operation Carlota was launched.

The first reinforcements arrived a few days later by plane—a battalion of special forces from the Interior Ministry. An artillery regiment came by ship.

The imperialist governments tried to justify their support to the South African invaders by holding the Soviet Union responsible for the Cuban internationalists sent to defend Angola. In fact, as Fidel has explained, Cuba's decision was an independent and sovereign action. It was after sending the first combatants, not before, that Cuba informed the Soviet Union.

Defeat of South African invasion

KOPPEL: What happened after the special forces of the Interior Ministry arrived?

VILLEGAS: At the same time that the South African troops were advancing from the south, the forces of Holden Roberto and Zairean soldiers were approaching Luanda from the north—they were within twenty-five kilometers [fifteen miles] from the capital. One day before independence was to be proclaimed, the battle of Quifangondo took place.

In Quifangondo, Cuban artillery units operated the six Soviet-made BM-21 multiple rocket launchers that had just come by sea. The special forces, who had arrived in Luanda a few hours earlier, were kept in reserve.

The BM-21 was a weapon the *Fenulas* (that was a pejorative term for the FNLA troops) had never seen before. The rocket fire shook them and they retreated in disarray.

That's how the FNLA was prevented from entering Luanda.

The next day, November 11, Neto proclaimed the independence of Angola, under an MPLA government. Big celebrations took place across the country.

At the same time a battle was unfolding in Cabinda, the oil-producing region, which had been invaded by the Zairean army. FAPLA forces and Cuban instructors, under the command of General Ramón Espinosa, drove the Zaireans from Cabinda.

Meanwhile, the FNLA fled toward their capital in the north, Carmona, which today is called Uíge. At the beginning of January 1976, Angolan and Cuban units under the command of General Víctor Schueg Colás launched an offensive in the north. They took Carmona and reached the border with Zaire. All the Zairean and FNLA forces were driven out of northern Angola.

It's important to note that in 1965 Schueg had been in the Congo with Che. The same year, as I mentioned earlier, Rafael Moracén had been in Congo-Brazzaville training MPLA guerrillas. Now, in 1975, Moracén was defending Angola in Cabinda. That's why I say that Che's column in the Congo and the column in Congo-Brazzaville laid the basis for our collaboration with the MPLA in the fight to defend Angola's independence ten years later.

Once the Zairean and FNLA forces were blocked from entering Luanda and were being pushed back in the north, what was most important was to prevent the South Africans from taking over Angola. Confronting Zaire was one thing, but confronting South Africa, with the strength and experience of its army, was a very different matter.

In November 1975, UNITA troops were advancing northward with the South Africans. But the South Africans were the real assault force that was opening the way. They came with armored personnel carriers, planes, and other equipment that was much more advanced than what UNITA had. When the South Africans "liberated" a town, UNITA would remain there as the occupation force and establish its "government."

Fighting took place in the central region in the final weeks of 1975. The Cuban special forces blocked the South African advance at Porto Amboim. Our forces, under the command of Díaz Argüelles, defeated the South Africans at Ebo and in other battles. Díaz Argüelles was killed December 11 in the battle of Catofe.

One of the most heroic battles took place in that area. Our combatants had retaken the Medunda hills from the South Africans. The South Africans and UNITA forces counterattacked. The enemy troops were right up against one of our infantry platoons. The platoon chief ordered his men to take cover in a cave and told our artillerymen, who were behind the hill, to fire on his position. The artillerymen hesitated. The platoon commander repeated the order. They opened

Mandela: The Cubans made an unparalleled contribution

The Cuban internationalists have made a contribution to African independence, freedom, and justice, unparalleled for its principled and selfless character. From its earliest days the Cuban Revolution has itself been a source of inspiration to all freedom-loving people. . . .

Where is the country that has sought Cuban help and has it refused? How many countries under threat from imperialism or struggling for national liberation have been able to count on Cuban support? . . .

We in Africa are used to being victims of countries wanting to carve up our territory or subvert our sovereignty. It is unparalleled in African history to have another people rise to the defense of one of us.

NELSON MANDELA
MATANZAS, CUBA
JULY 26, 1991

fire and the enemy had to retreat.

Thousands of Cuban soldiers continued to arrive in Angola. By the end of March 1976 the number had reached thirty-six thousand. Together with FAPLA they were able to defeat the South Africans and UNITA. The South African forces were driven out; the last South African troops crossed the border into Namibia on March 27, 1976.

This stage of the mission culminated with the consolidation of an independent Angola and a government led by the MPLA.

“Cuba’s internationalism in Africa begins with the first years of the revolution.”

TRICONTINENTAL

CASA EDITORA ABRIL

Top: Congo, 1965. Ernesto Che Guevara (right) and other Cuban volunteers who supported fight against proimperialist regime in that central African country.

Bottom: Congo-Brazzaville, March 1966. Cuban volunteers train MPLA guerrillas fighting Portuguese colonial rule in northern Angola. A decade later, Cuban help in defending Angola’s independence built on this collaboration.

"The victory in Guinea-Bissau detonated the 1974 revolution in Portugal. The new government ceded independence to all its African colonies."

COURTESY VÍCTOR DREKE

Top: Crowd in Lisbon celebrates overthrow of dictatorship in Portugal, April 1974. By November 1975, all Portuguese colonies in Africa had won independence.

Bottom: Cuban combatants in Guinea-Conakry near border with Guinea-Bissau, 1967. Víctor Dreke (second from left) led first group of Cuban internationalist volunteers aiding independence war against Portuguese rule in Guinea-Bissau.

CIENCIAS SOCIALES

In October 1975, South African troops invaded Angola from the south, while Zairean and US-backed FNLA troops invaded from the north. Cuba sent volunteer combatants to help defend the newly independent country. Together with the Angolan army, they expelled the invaders by March 1976.

Top: (From left) Cuban commanders Raúl Díaz Argüelles, René Hernández Gattorno, and Leopoldo Cintra Frías on battlefront near Porto Amboim, central Angola, November 1975. Díaz Argüelles commanded forces that blocked South African advance. He was killed in battle in December 1975. One in four Cubans who died in combat during Angolan mission was an officer.

Bottom: Luanda, November 11, 1976. Celebration of first anniversary of Angola's independence.

“There was a big difference between the FNLA, whose soldiers committed abuses, and our respectful treatment of civilians. That contributed greatly to winning over the population.”

VERDE OLIVO

In 1977-79 Villegas led unit of Cuban advisers working with the Angolan army in the north, where they defeated remnants of FNLA forces. **Top:** Harry Villegas (second from right), greets Angolan defense minister Iko Carreira and other Angolan leaders in northern town of Negage.

Bottom: Residents gather in Ambrizete, northwest Angola, after Cuban and Angolan forces expelled FNLA troops, January 1976.

CIENCIAS SOCIALES

"After the apartheid army was forced out of Angola in 1976, UNITA, backed by the South Africans, waged an irregular war for years."

VERDE OLIVO

The Angolan government organized irregular units to fight UNITA bands and asked Cuba for help. "Our leadership sent officers who had led the struggle that defeated counterrevolutionary bands in Cuba in the early years of the revolution," Villegas says. General Raúl Menéndez Tomassevich, who had won Angolans' respect, headed that effort.

Top: Combing operation against UNITA forces. **Bottom:** Tomassevich (right) greets Angolan president Agostinho Neto, late 1970s. Angola's defense minister, Iko Carreira, is on the left.

"I have full confidence in your unbreakable courage. I promise we will rescue you, whatever it takes."

—Fidel Castro

Message to Cuban and Angolan combatants resisting UNITA and South African siege of Cangamba, August 1983

VERDE OLIVO

VERDE OLIVO

On August 2, 1983, South African-backed UNITA troops attacked southeastern village of Cangamba. Heavily outnumbered FAPLA troops and Cuban advisers, short of food, water, and ammunition, withstood assault for a week. Fidel Castro's message "greatly raised morale," Villegas said.

VERDE OLIVO

This page, top: Wounded Cuban combatants being evacuated after encirclement of village was broken.

Opposite page, top: Cuban helicopter on support mission during battle. "From Menongue, we sent planes to provide air cover nonstop. Our pilots flew hundreds of missions."

Left: Cuban and Angolan combatants celebrate victory in Cangamba.

“The Cuban civilian mission helped to consolidate the Angolan economy. Thousands of Cubans were part of the coffee harvest in the early years. Some were truck drivers and stevedores who helped bring the crop to Luanda and load it onto ships.”

CUBAN INSTITUTE OF RADIO AND TELEVISION

During Cuba’s 16-year mission in Angola, in addition to 375,000 combatants some 50,000 volunteered as teachers, construction workers, medical personnel, and other essential tasks. Missions generally lasted two years.

EDITORA POLÍTICA

Top: Cuban instructors train Angolan truck drivers as part of reconstruction effort after 1975–76 war.

Bottom: Cuban volunteer teacher Lucía Matalón with students at home for orphaned children in Luanda.

UNITA and South Africa: The irregular war, 1976–87

WATERS: Your first mission to Angola was from March 1977 to mid-1979. What were your responsibilities?

VILLEGAS: By the time I arrived, the armies of Zaire and South Africa had already been driven out. In the north FAPLA was consolidating its positions. Our forces were protecting Angola against any threat of a new invasion by the regime in Zaire. There were still some FNLA troops there, but they no longer controlled cities, only some villages. From time to time they attacked a farm or small village. The FNLA was disintegrating. Most of the action took place in the area of Malanje.

I was given command of the Northern Motorized Infantry Regiment, the unit of Cuban advisers to FAPLA in the region that today includes the northern provinces of Uíge, Zaire, Cuanza Norte, and Malanje. Our headquarters was in the town of Negage, which in colonial days had been a Portuguese airbase.

We engaged in combat with the FNLA several times. I was wounded twice.

CALERO: Fidel and Raúl have often explained that during the revolutionary war in Cuba, civilians and soldiers of the Batista dictatorship captured by the Rebel Army were treated with respect. This has always been the political stance of the

Cuban leadership. What was your experience in Angola in that regard?

VILLEGAS: That was true in Angola as well. Many FNLA and Zairean soldiers chose to surrender to our forces because they knew we treated prisoners well. There was a big difference between the FNLA—the abuses they committed—and our respectful treatment of the civilian population. That contributed greatly to winning the population to the MPLA.

There was an incident in which a Cuban pilot mistakenly dropped bombs on a home in a *quimbo*, a hamlet, and some civilians were killed. Fidel insisted the pilot be tried in Angola under that country's laws. Neto said it hadn't been done deliberately; the pilot wasn't prosecuted.

Our government's stance was that Cubans involved in any such case be tried in Angola. It's the opposite of the US government. When the US intervenes in other countries it demands that its forces—which bomb and kill civilians with impunity—be given immunity.

Yes, the Cuban pilot made a mistake. But civilians had been killed.

Fidel gave the order that the pilot be withdrawn from the war. War starts to affect a person's psychology, he said. Your interaction with death can begin to lessen how you value life; you start getting accustomed to death. Fidel sought in every way to prevent us from becoming psychologically warped and turned into people for whom life had no value.

That was also one of the reasons that Fidel said we shouldn't be involved in a fratricidal war. He explained that Cuba's role was to defend Angola against foreign invasions. We would fight the South African army. We would have military advisers helping the Angolan forces. But it was FAPLA that would be fighting the UNITA and FNLA bands.

We weren't going to take part in a war among Angolans.

Nor could we allow our people to become desensitized to death, to be turned into killing machines.

I personally saw how the FNLA used the civilian population as human shields. On one occasion FAPLA was carrying out an offensive against FNLA bandits. I participated at the head of a battalion that advanced from Negage. We found that the bandits had taken the civilian population as hostages. They put women and children in front to prevent us from shooting. They knew that, with the human sensitivity revolutionaries have, we weren't going to fire on civilians. The FNLA took advantage of the time they gained and escaped down the river.

In another instance, a group of us were flying in two helicopters. The FNLA hit the first one with machine gun fire and it crashed against some trees. I was in the second helicopter and we landed to look for our comrades. But night was already falling and we couldn't find them. When we returned the next day, we found all fifteen bodies had been cut up with machetes by the FNLA.

Afterward we launched a defensive operation with several Cuban and FAPLA battalions that destroyed the FNLA bases in the Uíge area.

Attempted coup against President Agostinho Neto

WATERS: In May 1977, a little after you arrived in Angola, there was an unsuccessful attempt to overthrow the government of Agostinho Neto. It was organized by MPLA leader Nito Alves. What happened and what was the response of the Cuban internationalists?

VILLEGAS: Nito Alves was minister of the interior and the MPLA organizer. He had a faction within the MPLA, and he placed his people in all the provinces as political commissars and in other leadership positions. The FAPLA chief of staff,

Monstro Imortal [Jacob Caetano João], and other MPLA leaders were also part of the coup. FAPLA's Ninth Brigade joined the Nito Alves revolt. The coup plotters took over the national radio station, the police headquarters, the prisons, and other targets in the capital.

The coup leaders took advantage of a weakness in the capital due to events two months earlier stemming from an invasion of Katanga, a province of Zaire, by a group of exiled Katangans based in Angola. The Katangans launched actions across the border to promote a secessionist movement in that Zairean province. At Mobutu's request, and with US and French backing, the Moroccan government sent a unit of troops to Zaire to defend the Mobutu regime. The Katangan exile forces were driven back into Angola.

To defend Angola and prevent Zairean troops from crossing the border, we sent an infantry regiment led by General Enrique Acevedo from Luanda toward the east.

As a result, fewer Cuban troops were participating in the defense of Luanda when Nito Alves's supporters launched their coup. The few Cuban units remaining included the group of advisers, headed by Rafael Moracén, who were part of the presidential guard.

In coordination with the Cuban command in Luanda, our personnel drove the coup plotters out of all the sites they had seized. Under Moracén's command, a unit from the presidential guard took back the national radio station. Moracén grabbed the microphone and announced that Neto was still the president—in the heat of the moment he spoke in Spanish.

The coup was defeated that day, practically without bloodshed. Afterward Cuban advisers accompanied FAPLA as they arrested those who had joined the revolt. In some provinces we had to give some backbone to FAPLA military commanders who were beginning to wobble. The commander in Carmona got weak in the knees. I brought him to the headquarters of the Cuban regiment to protect him until the coup plotters had been captured.

Nito Alves escaped and headed north. A few weeks later a group of Cuban advisers to the Ministry of the Interior found him and turned him over to the government.

WATERS: What was behind the coup? What were the political differences between Alves and the Neto leadership?

VILLEGAS: It was the thirst for power. Nito Alves wanted to replace Neto. As far as I know, it wasn't because of ideological differences. But he felt that the Soviets sympathized with him, and that emboldened him to act.

The struggle against UNITA

CALERO: After the first invasion was defeated and operations were under way to drive the FNLA out of the north, what was going on in other parts of the country?

VILLEGAS: The South African army withdrew from Angola in March 1976, but the covert war continued. South African instructors infiltrated to train UNITA troops in southern Angola. They were also training them in northern Namibia. UNITA kept up its attacks.

In response to this situation, the Regiment for Struggle against Mercenary Bands was formed. It was headquartered in Huambo in the central region, and collaborated with FAPLA in operations against UNITA. In southern Angola we had regular troops, whose task was to protect the country against South African incursions.

Soon after I arrived in Angola in 1977, General Raúl Menéndez Tomassevich took charge as head of our military mission. Over the next two years FAPLA, accompanied by Cuban advisers, went on the offensive against UNITA, preventing them from controlling any important positions.

UNITA was a stronger enemy than the FNLA. They were a well-organized guerrilla army, with money and weapons from the South African and US governments. In each region under their control they had both a military structure and a government structure. They created a network of roads.

At one point UNITA controlled some big diamond mines in Lucapa, in Lunda Norte province. They sent the diamonds directly to Europe from an airport there. Diamond mining generated a lot of income for them.

UNITA, as I mentioned, was based among the Ovimbundu, the largest ethnic group in parts of central Angola. In his struggle for power, Savimbi promoted reactionary policies. He spoke of creating a "black state" in Angola. He criticized the MPLA for including not only blacks but Angolans of mixed race and whites in its ranks. The MPLA sought to go beyond the ethnic divisions, giving it a broader base of support than UNITA.

Savimbi would even assert that UNITA was fighting for a "black socialist republic," and that Cuba backed the MPLA because of "geographic fatalism." He claimed that if he had made contact with us first, he would have sided with Cuba, but since Neto allied with Cuba first, he had no choice but to ally himself with South Africa.

UNITA allied itself with reactionary forces, just as the FNLA did. Savimbi was a tool of imperialism. During the fight for independence, he had collaborated with the Portuguese in their attacks against the MPLA.

In fact, UNITA didn't have a defined ideology. That's why when they arrived in an area, people didn't join them, so they recruited by force. They would arrive at a village, look for the young men, and take them away. A youth was given a rifle and trained to shoot. With that he became a member.

Supported by the South African army, UNITA waged an irregular war. The South Africans created the 32nd Battalion, the so-called Buffalo Battalion. It was an elite unit with South African officers but made up mostly of Angolans. Many of them had been in the FNLA and took refuge in Namibia after the FNLA was defeated.

From its bases in Namibia, the Buffalo Battalion penetrated more deeply into Angola than other units of the South African special forces. It carried out many massacres in Angolan villages and pursued the guerrilla fighters of SWAPO, the South West Africa People's Organisation.

SWAPO was fighting for the independence of Namibia, which had been a colony of South Africa since they took it over from Germany at the end of World War I. SWAPO had bases in southern Angola and would cross the border to carry out operations in Namibia. The South African government justified its military actions in Angola by arguing they were fighting SWAPO.

The Cassinga massacre

The town of Cassinga, in southern Angola, housed a Namibian refugee camp, protected by a very small force of SWAPO fighters. The South Africans claimed it was an important SWAPO military base. Using that as a pretext, South African forces carried out a massacre in Cassinga in May 1978. They bombed the town and killed six hundred Namibians, many of them children, women, and elderly.

In response, one of our units nearby, with tanks and artillery, was quickly deployed toward Cassinga to defend the Namibians. South African planes attacked this unit at their most vulnerable moment, as they were moving. Sixteen Cuban combatants were killed there. It was the first time Cubans and Namibians shed their blood together.

The imperialist press agencies said practically nothing about the Cassinga massacre.

This led to the decision that each Cuban brigade would have a designated area within which it could respond independently, without asking for authorization. If a UNITA band entered that area, it was the job of the Cuban unit to expel it. Unless they were attacked, Cuban soldiers didn't engage in combat with UNITA. That was done by FAPLA.

CALERO: During the time you were in Angola, Cuba was not only contributing to the military defense of Angola. In addition to 375,000 combatants, over the sixteen years of the internationalist mission another 50,000 Cubans served as civilian workers. They helped throughout the country as teachers, construction workers, medical personnel, and in other areas. What was their role in the northern region where you were at that time?

VILLEGAS: In the early years the Cuban civilian mission helped consolidate the Angolan economy. In the northern region, for example, they played an important role in the coffee harvest.

Coffee is one of Angola's major export crops, and there are coffee plantations—*fazendas*—all across the northern mountains. When I traveled through the mountains on the road to Luanda, I would pass through a white sea of flowering coffee plants—a beautiful sight.

Because of the war, the coffee harvest hadn't been taken to Luanda for export. It had been accumulating in warehouses. There were few drivers and agricultural technicians, since those jobs had been done by Portuguese and they had left Angola.

Thousands of Cubans helped with the coffee harvest. Some of our soldiers became truck drivers and stevedores, helping to get the harvest to Luanda and on board ships.

We also had to provide protection for the Cuban civilian volunteers, who were targeted by FNLA and UNITA bandits. Volunteers were dispersed over wide areas—a house over here, a coffee plantation over there. Each plantation had a self-defense system, and all the self-defense systems worked jointly.

But many times our military units had to evacuate them. One time our intelligence informed us that a group of bandits was planning to attack all the fazendas in the north where there were Cubans. We organized a big operation and got all the Cuban volunteers out of there for a while.

WATERS: When you returned to Cuba in 1979, what were your responsibilities?

VILLEGAS: Based on an apparent improvement in the military situation, in early 1979, in agreement with the Angolan government, Cuba withdrew its advisers from FAPLA units. In southern Angola the Cuban forces pulled back from the Namibian border area and established a strong defense line that ran from the port of Namibe to Menongue. That line was about 250 kilometers north of the border. Its purpose was to protect against any advance by South African troops.

A few months later Tomassevich returned to Cuba, and so did I. For the following two years I commanded the regiment of motorized infantry in the FAR's Tank Division.

KOPPEL: When Cuba withdrew its military advisers, Soviet advisers to FAPLA remained, but clearly there were frictions. Lúcio Lara, one of the central Angolan leaders, commented on this during a meeting with Cuban leaders in Havana in December 1981. The military recommendations of the Soviet advisers are "well beyond our capabilities," he said, "and, frankly, not relevant to the real situation in Angola. Their officers have no experience of guerrilla warfare. They see everything through a conventional prism. . . . They say that something can be done in twenty-four hours, but we need six days, or a week. We don't have the airplanes, or we have the plane and we don't have the fuel. . . . The Cuban experience is far more relevant and therefore, for us, of decisive importance."*

Fidel has talked about differences too. How did the Cuban leadership see the challenges faced in Angola?

VILLEGAS: The Soviet advisers proposed that Angola build up a conventional army, equipped with tanks and heavy weapons, to defend themselves from South Africa.

Fidel said yes, the South African army was Angola's main enemy, but FAPLA didn't have the military capability to confront the South Africans. Cuba would take on the task of defending Angola from South African attacks, he insisted, and FAPLA should concentrate on the war against UNITA.

For that they didn't need a conventional army. They needed units with light equipment, trained for irregular warfare.

In 1979–80, influenced by the Soviet advisers, FAPLA pulled back from operations against UNITA and concentrated on training regular army units. UNITA, with South African and US support, began to recover and grow.

In 1981 the Angolan government again asked Cuba to provide military advisers for FAPLA. For that responsibility our leadership chose officers who had participated in the *Lucha Contra Bandidos* (Struggle against Bandits) in Cuba, the operation during the early years of the revolution when we defeated the US-backed counterrevolutionary bands in the Escambray mountains. Many of these officers had served previously in Angola. We shared our experiences with the Angolans.

* Quoted in Piero Gleijeses, *Visions of Freedom* (Chapel Hill: University of North Carolina Press, 2013), pp. 194–95.

That's how what was known as *Operación Olivo* began. Tomassevich returned to Angola to command it. The name *Olivo* [olive drab] eventually came to identify all the Cuban combatants who served as advisers in the fight against UNITA over the following decade.

Of necessity, the fight against the UNITA bandits was irregular warfare. For that purpose FAPLA organized the light infantry brigades, which had Cuban advisers—that was *Operación Olivo*. The Soviet advisers remained with the regular Angolan army units.

WATERS: Why was Tomassevich chosen?

VILLEGAS: Tomassevich had been commander of the *Lucha Contra Bandidos* in Cuba. Also, when he headed the Cuban military mission in Angola from 1977 to 1979, he had won the respect of the Angolans. He got along with them very well.

WATERS: Around the time Tomassevich returned to Cuba in 1981, you began your second mission in Angola. What were your new responsibilities?

'Had to set an example'

VILLEGAS: In Havana there was a special command post for our military missions abroad, headed by Fidel. At the time, that included Angola, Ethiopia, and Nicaragua. In mid-1981 I was assigned to be the liaison between the special command post in Havana and the command for *Operación Olivo*. I flew back and forth between Cuba and Angola constantly.

Fidel insisted that the Cuban advisers in the Angolan units had to exercise their influence through their conduct and example at all times, day and night. They had to live side by side with the FAPLA troops and be ready to engage in combat along with their battalion if attacked.

In the field, our advisers worked shoulder to shoulder with the Angolan soldiers. They shared the same difficult conditions and dangers. At night, however, they tended to cluster together near the Cuban command center, instead of sleeping with their Angolan units. Even though they were instructed not to, they kept doing it. They felt safer that way, more able to repel an attack if they had to.

Fidel demanded that end. Cuban forces were to sleep alongside the troops they were advising. He said they were acting like chicks around a mother hen, taking cover under the hen's wings at night.

As in all else, Fidel said, the Cubans had to set an example.

In this our approach was different from that of the Soviet advisers. In 1965, when we were involved in the struggle in the Congo under Che's command, our conduct clashed with that of the guerrillas who'd been trained in Bulgaria. The Bulgarians—and other Soviet-allied Communist Parties—acted in line with what they called "cadre preservation." They trained their Congolese cadres not to go into combat. They were to be "preserved" so in the future, when it came time to take power, they would become the country's leaders.

For us it's different. A leader has to set the example, has to fight. That doesn't mean sacrificing yourself and getting killed unnecessarily. But yes, when the hour for combat arrives, a leader has to be at the front of his troops.

That's why Fidel has so much authority. He didn't tell combatants "Go!"—he'd say, "Let's go!" He was always at the front. He led the attack on the Moncada barracks in 1953, just as he was at the front at Playa Girón.

In Angola our officers led their troops. One of every four Cubans who died in combat was an officer.

The battle of Cangamba

WATERS: In the early 1980s, as you've described, the attacks by UNITA forces intensified, as did raids by the South African army. One of the most important battles took place in August 1983 at Cangamba, in southeastern Angola. You were involved in that battle, where Cuban and Angolan soldiers managed to resist the numerically superior enemy forces. How did it unfold?

VILLEGAS: At that time UNITA, with increased backing from the South African and US governments, was growing stronger. They had penetrated deep into Angolan territory and were planning to march to the northeast.

Their goal was to take Luena, the capital of Moxico province in the center-eastern region. That city would have given them control of the railroad that provided a link to the neighboring countries of Zaire and Zambia. The first step was to attack Cangamba and other towns in Moxico in order to isolate Luena. If they could take control of Cangamba, they thought, they could also capture the Cuban advisers and display them to the international press.

Through these moves UNITA was also aiming to take over territory further north—the diamond-rich provinces of Lunda Norte and Lunda Sur.

On August 2, 1983, UNITA troops attacked Cangamba with

heavy artillery and mortar fire. The town was defended by a brigade of 818 men—FAPLA's 32nd Light Infantry Brigade—and ninety-two Cuban advisers. UNITA had deployed some three thousand troops, supported by South African army advisers and special forces. They had the town surrounded.

The situation in Cangamba was very complex for FAPLA and for us. It was a hard-to-reach area, 250 kilometers from Menongue, the nearest city from which we could provide air cover and reinforcements.

That same day, August 2, General Leopoldo Cintra Frías—everyone knows him as Polo—returned to Angola from Cuba. I accompanied him. Polo, who earlier had been head of our troops in southern Angola, was the new chief of the Cuban military mission.

We had gone to Havana to discuss some leadership changes in Angola. Polo was proposing to establish a forward command post in Huambo, in the central part of the country, and that he go there with other officers in order to be closer to the combat zones. That would leave only a small Cuban operational group in Luanda, where FAPLA had its general headquarters.

Fidel disagreed. The most important thing for Polo was to remain with the FAPLA leaders, elbow to elbow, not apart from them, Fidel explained. We had to analyze all the problems together with the Angolans, not leave them to sort things out alone in Luanda with the Soviet advisers. And Fidel was right.

When we got to the Luanda airport, General Enrique Lussón, commander of *Operación Olivo* at that time, and General Amels Escalante, chief of staff of the mission, briefed Polo on the situation in Cangamba. Polo immediately sent reinforcements by helicopter, some hundred combatants.

Two armored columns were also dispatched, one from

Huambo and another from Menongue, to reinforce the defense of Cangamba. It was a long, slow trek since they had to cross territory occupied by UNITA troops and try to avoid landmines along the roads.

UNITA launched one assault after another on Cangamba. Their troops were able to occupy parts of the town.

The battle lasted a week. FAPLA and the Cubans were surrounded. They were running low on ammunition, water, and food. The defensive perimeter gradually shrank down to the size of a soccer field. UNITA took all the positions where there were sources of water.

From Menongue we sent planes to provide air cover for the troops. Nonstop. One plane was heading to Cangamba while another was returning to the base. Our pilots flew hundreds of missions.

We had to fire on some little houses that separated our people from the UNITA troops. But it was difficult for our pilots to drop bombs on the enemy troops since they were so close to ours.

As I mentioned earlier, throughout the war the Cuban combatants had always set an example of how much we valued human lives. One example of the progress we made could be seen in Cangamba when, as a result of our joint work over the years, FAPLA soldiers began to bring back and bury the bodies of their own who had died on the battlefield, as we do. That wasn't a common practice in Angola or in wars in Africa in general. Armies would leave the bodies behind and the birds of prey would eat them. It showed we'd made important progress.

At a certain point in the battle of Cangamba, our planes had used up all their C-5 missiles. We had asked the Soviets for more, but they kept delaying. Our leadership decided to use our reserve supply in Cuba and send them to Angola. It would have taken too long by ship, so Fidel ordered the seats stripped out of an IL-62 airliner to turn it into a transport plane for the missiles. That way the C-5s arrived in Luanda quickly. The warplanes were already on the landing strip. They were loaded with the missiles and flown to Menongue, so our pilots were able to use them at Cangamba.

Our arsenal was running out, so soldiers began using weapons they devised themselves: incendiary bombs dropped from planes as well as other rudimentary weapons to stop the enemy's advance. It was a bloody, difficult battle.

The desperation among our troops in Cangamba had reached the point where Polo decided to give the order to break out of the encirclement.

Fidel was closely following the combat; he was in communication with Polo on a daily basis. When Polo reported he had given this order, Fidel said it was a big mistake because UNITA bandits dominated the surrounding terrain.

'Whatever it takes'

That's when Fidel sent a message to the Cubans and to FAPLA's 32nd Brigade in Cangamba. The leadership of the revolution would not abandon them, he told them. Two powerful armored columns were on their way to back them up. They should resist no matter what until reinforcements arrived.

"I'm confident in your unshakable courage," Fidel said. "I promise we will rescue you, whatever it takes."

KOPPEL: What was the impact of Fidel's message on the soldiers in Cangamba?

VILLEGAS: It was tremendous. It raised the morale of the combatants enormously. They held out more than a week, virtually without food, water, or reinforcements. It was heroic.

By then, the bombardment by our pilots was inflicting heavy casualties on UNITA. On August 9 they decided to retreat.

Message to Cuban and Angolan combatants in Cangamba

We have followed hour by hour your heroic resistance in Cangamba confronting South African puppet forces far superior in number and military means. We have taken all measures to support you.

The Cuban reinforcements arriving by helicopter confirm our determination to win this battle. Powerful armored columns are now advancing rapidly toward Cangamba.

Now everything depends on your capacity to resist as long as necessary for these troops to reach their destination.

Calmly, self-confidently, you must repel the enemy attacks. You need to save ammunition, fire accurately, and withstand hunger and thirst if provisions and water run out.

All means will be used to free you from the siege. Our troops will arrive in three to four days. But if obstacles delay them, you have to resist, because they will arrive, whatever it takes.

Let Cangamba become an example showing that the blood Angolans and Cubans have shed for the freedom and dignity of Africa has not been in vain.

I have full confidence in your unbreakable courage. I promise we will rescue you, whatever it takes.

COMMANDER IN CHIEF FIDEL CASTRO
AUGUST 7, 1983

Our two armored columns still hadn't arrived because of all the obstacles they were encountering on the way. After

UNITA pulled back, these columns were redeployed, one to Luena and the other back to Menongue.

Eighteen Cubans and sixty FAPLA fighters died in combat. UNITA lost hundreds of soldiers.

One of the Cubans killed was Major Policarpo Álvarez Pileta, a pilot and former Rebel Army combatant. At one point we had lost track of the position of the column coming from Menongue, so Polo sent two helicopters to locate it. Policarpo and I were in one of them.

When we saw a road in the forest, our helicopter flew a little lower to reconnoiter. Policarpo spotted some trucks and said, "There's UNITA."

Our orders were to locate the Cuban column, I pointed out, not to engage UNITA at that moment. Besides, our helicopter wasn't armed with rockets. We couldn't defend ourselves.

"I didn't come here to run away from UNITA," Policarpo replied. "I came to fight them."

We decided our helicopter would swoop down while the other stayed above. The enemy began to shoot, and Policarpo returned fire. It turned out to be a nest of antiaircraft batteries, and he was hit by a bullet. We flew him to Menongue but he died. I asked for air support, and a couple of MIG-21s destroyed that UNITA encampment.

On August 11, after UNITA had retreated, Fidel ordered us to leave Cangamba the same day. He was certain South African planes would retaliate for UNITA's defeat.

Polo proposed the withdrawal to Angolan president José dos Santos and the FAPLA command. But the head of the Soviet military mission, General Konstantin Kurochkin, argued for the opposite. He insisted in the meeting that FAPLA take advantage of the victory to mount an offensive from Cangamba toward the southwest. The Angolans decided to remain there.

When Fidel learned of the Angolan decision, he sent an urgent cable to Polo, telling him to try to convince the Angolan government it would be a serious error to keep its forces in Cangamba, and we should evacuate our people immediately. "We can't allow a victory to be turned into a setback," he said.

After we retreated, things unfolded just as Fidel had predicted. Two days later, the South African air force came in. They bombed and destroyed Cangamba. FAPLA retreated, but now with many casualties. UNITA occupied what was left of the town.

WATERS: The divergent courses advocated by the Soviet advisers and by the Cuban leadership were evident on other occasions, weren't they?

VILLEGAS: The fundamental divergences over the war weren't with the Angolans, who played a passive role in this debate, but with the Soviets. These disagreements came to the fore many times, culminating with the final battle at Cuito Cuanavale in 1987–88.

When UNITA stepped up attacks in central Angola in mid-1983, their Second Front captured the town of Mussende, in Cuanza Sul province. The Soviet advisers proposed FAPLA launch a major offensive to take back the town, as you would in conventional warfare.

They supplied maps showing very complicated operations with a lot of big arrows. When Fidel heard about this plan, he derided it as "Operation Berlin."

CALERO: Why?

VILLEGAS: Because it wasn't Berlin.

The Battle of Berlin during World War II was a massive operation in which hundreds of thousands of Soviet troops advanced on the German capital. The Soviet advisers in Angola described the plans to retake this town as if they were

Fidel Castro: Soviet advisers thought it was the Battle of Berlin

The Soviet advisers in Luanda were recommending offensives against far-away targets in southeast Angola—against the bandits' supposed general command and headquarters, far from all sources of supplies. They were absurd, ill-conceived military operations. We categorically opposed them and did not participate.

The Soviets thought they were fighting the Battle of Berlin again, with thousands of tanks, forty thousand heavy artillery pieces, and Marshal Zhukov at the helm. They had an academic mentality, trained in the purest style of conventional warfare. They didn't understand, nor could they understand, the problems of the Third World and the kind of war that had to be waged under those conditions.

We would tell the Soviets, "If you want the Angolans to carry out such offensives, you must first block South Africa's interventions." We said this over and over for three, four, five years, until there was a serious military crisis [in 1987], when the South African army penetrated deep inside the Republic of Angola to try to destroy it.

At that moment we had to make the most difficult decision, practically staking the revolution itself. We assessed what was necessary to stop South Africa's interference and finally defeat it. We decided to send from Cuba all the troops and equipment required. It was then that the famous battle of Cuito Cuanavale took place.

FIDEL CASTRO
KINGSTON, JAMAICA
JULY 30, 1998

Marshal Zhukov presenting the offensive against Berlin to Stalin in 1945.

But the struggle against UNITA required irregular warfare, with light units.

Our approach was to defeat the enemy through an accumulation of small victories, not through an "Ayacucho." Ayacucho, in what is now Peru, was the final decisive battle of the South American independence wars, where Spain's royalist troops were resoundingly defeated in 1824 by the pro-independence forces.

Another important battle took place in March 1984, when UNITA attacked Sumbe, the capital of Cuanza Sul. In Sumbe there were no regular FAPLA troops, only three hundred militia members. There were also 230 Cuban civilian volunteers, along with Italian, Portuguese, Soviet, and Bulgarian civilian workers. UNITA's aim was to capture the city and hold hostage a large number of foreign aid workers.

Despite the enemy's military superiority—they had fifteen hundred troops—the Cuban construction workers, teachers, and health workers fought heroically with the weapons they had. Together with the Angolan militia, they defended Sumbe until the Cuban planes arrived and UNITA was repelled. Cuban pilots also achieved a truly heroic feat: since they had no direct phone communication with Sumbe, they had to call Luanda and get information from there.

Among the ninety who died in battle in Sumbe were seven

Cuban workers. The enemy suffered heavy casualties.

As UNITA, backed by the South Africans, stepped up attacks in the central provinces in the mid-1980s, they blew up bridges and hydroelectric dams. Fidel saw they were creating conditions to isolate Luanda. The assault on Cangamba showed the danger. In response, we reinforced our troop levels in Angola from twenty-five thousand to thirty-nine thousand.

Fidel gave instructions for Cuban soldiers, in mixed Angolan-Cuban units, to occupy every strategic bridge on the roads to Luanda and all the hydroelectric dams. That prevented UNITA from isolating Luanda by land and depriving it of electric power.

Had to live like moles

South Africa had a network of military bases along the Namibian side of Angola's southern border. Its planes carried out aerial assaults and controlled the skies in southern Angola. To counter this, we reinforced our defense line, which went from Namibe to Menongue. To protect themselves from the South African raids, our soldiers on that line lived like moles—most of the time they were underground.

The Soviet advisers maintained their "Battle of Berlin" strategy. For years they'd been trying to convince the Angolan leadership they had to strike a decisive blow to UNITA and the South African forces at Mavinga, a remote town in Cuando Cubango province in the southeast.

If FAPLA took Mavinga, the Soviets insisted, they could then launch an offensive against Jamba, Savimbi's headquarters. Jamba was in a forested area in the far southeast corner of Angola, near the borders with Namibia and Zambia.

But Mavinga was a trap. It was far from Menongue, the nearest supply point, we pointed out to the Angolans. UNITA, on the other hand, could be resupplied from the other side of the border and retreat there when necessary. Besides, the South Africans could launch a crushing air attack against forces advancing on Mavinga.

This was debated among the Angolans, Soviets, and Cubans for the better part of 1984 and 1985. In meetings with the Angolan leadership, Polo insisted that the central region was where it was more important for FAPLA to defeat UNITA. That area was much more decisive economically and militarily than the border province of Cuando Cubango.

Nonetheless, General Konstantin Kurochkin, the chief of the Soviet advisers, convinced the Angolan leaders to attack Mavinga.

In mid-1985 the Angolans initiated Operation Second Congress—named after the second congress of the MPLA. Some six thousand FAPLA troops advanced, at first without problems. Suddenly, the South African fighter planes and artillery began to pound them, massively. The FAPLA soldiers resisted heroically but had to retreat. Nearly two thousand Angolan soldiers died.

WATERS: In his interview with Ignacio Ramonet,* Fidel says the US government, through Israel, had transferred to the South African regime several atomic bombs similar to those used in Hiroshima and Nagasaki. In planning military strategy, the Cuban leadership took into account the possibility these weapons could be used against Cuban and Angolan troops. Fidel explains that Cuba avoided large concentrations of troops in order to minimize loss of life if the South African forces employed that arsenal.

VILLEGAS: Our high command knew the South Africans had several nuclear weapons that could be used in the theater of

* Fidel Castro, *My Life*, edited by Ignacio Ramonet (London: Penguin Books, 2007).

operations. We now know they had six such weapons, provided by the US through the Israeli government.

In Angola our military forces were organized in tactical groups of not more than a thousand soldiers. That is, there were no large concentrations of forces they could devastate with a single blow.

Cuito Cuanavale, Calueque, and defeat of the apartheid regime, 1987–91

WATERS: After Cangamba, and in face of growing South African threats, the Cuban leadership decided to strengthen your forces in Angola, as you explained earlier. This was done despite the dangers Cuba faced with Washington's military escalation in Central America and the Caribbean.

In October 1983, two months after Cangamba, US armed forces invaded and occupied Grenada. Washington was already organizing and financing the "Contra" war against the revolutionary government in Nicaragua. It was supporting bloody dictatorships in El Salvador and Guatemala and carrying out large-scale military maneuvers in Caribbean waters.

At the same time, however, mass protests against apartheid were growing among workers and youth across South Africa. The political crisis in Pretoria was deepening. In October 1985, Fidel had a meeting in Havana with Soviet foreign minister Eduard Shevardnadze. After a decade of South African invasions and military operations, Fidel argued, it was time to "cut off the hands" of the apartheid regime inside Angola.

A year later, in a September 1986 speech in Luanda, Fidel pledged that Cuba was "willing to maintain its internationalist troops in Angola as long as apartheid exists."

Then, in November 1986, the Iran-Contra scandal broke

open, dealing a blow to the credibility of the US government. White House officials, it was revealed, were secretly organizing weapons sales to Iran in order to secure release of hostages held by Tehran's Hezbollah allies in Lebanon, and the money was being siphoned to fund the counterrevolutionary forces in Nicaragua.

Fidel correctly concluded that the moment was more favorable than ever to "cut off the hands" of Pretoria. How did this unfold?

VILLEGAS: In mid-1987 FAPLA launched an offensive called "Operation Salute to October," referring to the seventieth anniversary of the October Revolution in Russia. The aim was to capture Savimbi's headquarters in Jamba.

Our leadership had opposed this Soviet-proposed offensive. It was a repetition of the 1985 Mavinga operation, which had been such a disaster.

FAPLA deployed four elite brigades with eleven thousand soldiers. At first they met little resistance from UNITA, which had about eight thousand soldiers in the area. But the South African army had anticipated the offensive and was supporting UNITA with hundreds of troops from its special forces.

The South Africans unleashed intense aerial and artillery attacks on FAPLA. The Angolan soldiers fought courageously but suffered heavy losses. One brigade was annihilated as it crossed the Lomba River. The remaining FAPLA troops retreated to the small town of Cuito Cuanavale, their southernmost base in Cuando Cubango province. The South Africans pursued them with the goal of taking Cuito.

In mid-November, after receiving a report on the critical situation in southern Angola, Fidel met with the FAR command. He asked: Are we going to let the South Africans destroy them, or are we going to help them? We've been supporting Angola for more than ten years, but now, within a

November 1987–April 1988

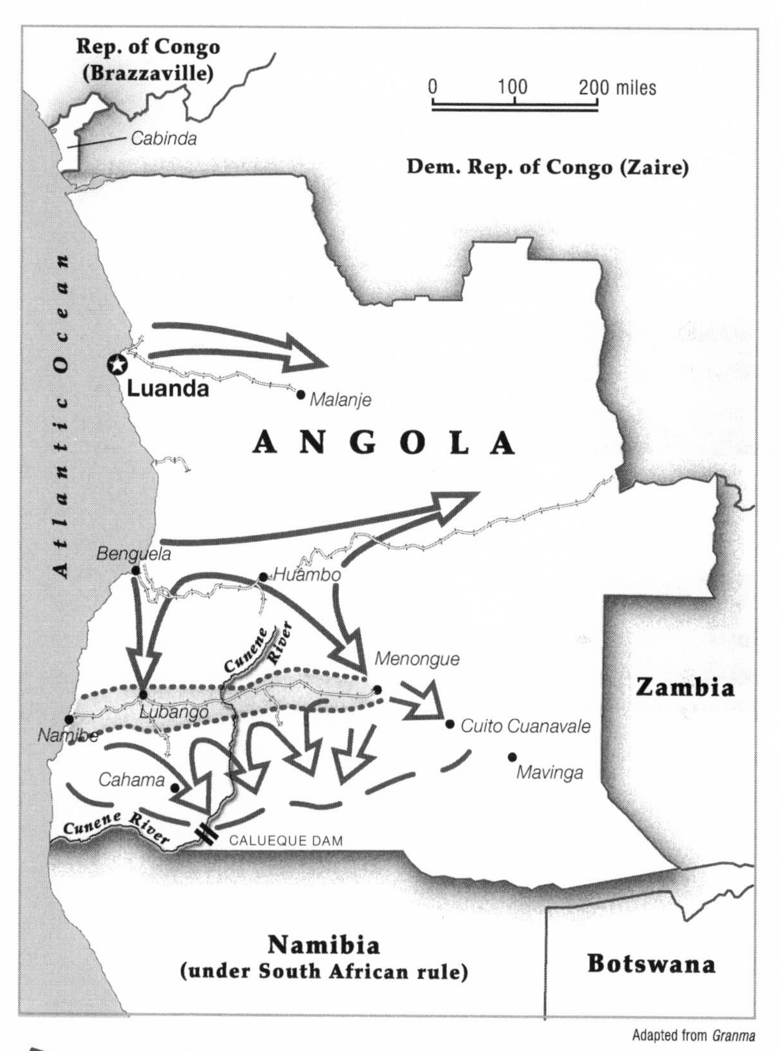

Adapted from *Granma*

Arrows denote movement of Cuban-Angolan-SWAPO forces

Cuban troop positions, November 1987

Forward position of Cuban-Angolan-SWAPO troops, April 1988

short time, all could be lost.

The decision was made to assemble a Cuban force that was large enough and well-enough equipped to decisively defeat the South Africans and drive them out of Angola. To achieve this, Fidel insisted, we had to control the skies in the south.

We increased our forces to more than fifty thousand. We sent hundreds of tanks and thousands of artillery pieces. Our best pilots. Our most modern planes, anti-aircraft weapons, and tanks.

In strengthening our forces we had a double objective: first, a defensive action to prevent Cuito's fall, and second, an offensive action in southwest Angola.

Our forces moved, as Fidel put it, like a boxer who blocks the blow with the left hand and strikes with the right.

KOPPEL: How was collaboration between the Cuban forces and SWAPO combatants organized during this strategic offensive?

VILLEGAS: SWAPO had bases in southwest Angola. From there they carried out combat operations in northern Namibia.

SWAPO collaborated with us in Angola not as combat troops but primarily as reconnaissance units. We conducted joint SWAPO-Cuban patrols near the Namibian border.

SWAPO troops played an important role in scouting missions that required a solid familiarity with the terrain, and they *did* know it well. They'd go deep into Namibe and Cunene provinces to see what the South Africans were doing in the areas they illegally controlled.

In the final stages of the war, when our troops were advancing in large numbers toward the border, SWAPO fighters accompanied them and played an important role.

Our people had confidence in the SWAPO guerrillas. They were brave, self-sacrificing fighters who had withstood heavy repression. The Namibian and Cuban combatants had warm human relations; they practically became one. It helped that Cuban soldiers were known for communicating readily with others, for learning the local languages, for mixing in with Angolans and Namibians.

CALERO: As events unfolded in the opening months of 1988, South African and US officials realized that the Angolan and Cuban forces advancing in the southwest were strong enough to drive all the way into Namibia.

In one of Pretoria's internal documents that later became public, one of their generals warned that if the South African military engaged in direct combat with the Cuban forces in southwest Angola, they risked losing their entire air force within a few days.

VILLEGAS: Cuba sent everything that was needed to Angola. That's true. If necessary, Raúl said, we'd go without underpants.

Tens of thousands of Cuban and Angolan troops, along with SWAPO combatants, were advancing toward the Namibian border. The South Africans saw the number of tanks, aircraft, and antiaircraft weapons we had in that one limited theater of operations. The Americans also noticed the number of ships leaving from Cuba with reinforcements.

Our airbase in Lubango was far from the Namibian border. So, in just ten weeks, a contingent of Cuban construction workers built an airfield in Cahama, almost on the border. That allowed our aircraft to reach all of southern Angola and enter northern Namibia.

Our MIG pilots gained control of the airspace.

As Fidel put it, we built up a force that was not only strong enough to enter Namibia but might not stop until it reached Pretoria.

The blows we dealt the South African army shattered the

GRANMA

After defeats suffered at Cuito Cuanavale and in southwest Angola in first half of 1988, South African government sued for peace. Accords signed at United Nations in New York, December 1988, ended South African intervention and recognized Namibia's independence.

At table, left to right: South African defense minister Magnus Malan and foreign minister Pik Botha; UN secretary-general Javier Pérez de Cuéllar; US secretary of state George Shultz; Angolan foreign minister Afonso Van-Dúnem; Angolan ambassador to US António dos Santos França; Cuban foreign minister Isidoro Malmierca; and Cuban general Abelardo Colomé.

We defeated the South Africans with minimum casualties

In Cuito Cuanavale the South Africans really broke their teeth. And it all came about with a minimum of casualties—a minimum of casualties!—for our own forces, the Angolan and Cuban forces.

The main idea was to stop them at Cuito Cuanavale and deal them blows from the southwest. Enough troops were gathered to seriously threaten points of strategic importance for South Africa and strike hard at them on terrain that we, not the enemy, had chosen.

We not only sent our best pilots to Angola, we also sent our best antiaircraft weapons, a large amount of mobile antiaircraft equipment, a good quantity of antiaircraft missile artillery. We reinforced our air power and we sent as many tanks, armored troop carriers, and artillery pieces as were needed.

FIDEL CASTRO
DECEMBER 5, 1988

morale of their troops. When they attacked us at Tchipa, in the southwest, our MIGS launched a counterattack near the Calueque Dam, almost on the border, that left the South Africans with heavy casualties and damage.

"The MIG-23S broke our hearts," a South African soldier wrote on a bridge there. That tells you how demoralized they'd become.

Cuito Cuanavale and Calueque were the two main victories that decided the war's outcome. We relied on deterrence. The war was won without big military confrontations. The South African government was afraid of suffering heavy casualties because of the political repercussions of the war at home.

The victories in Cuito Cuanavale and southwest Angola forced the South Africans to come to the negotiating table. After we defeated them on the battlefield, they agreed to withdraw their forces and accept the independence of Namibia.

By the end of August 1988, all South African troops had been pulled out of Angola. In December of that year, the governments of South Africa, Angola, and Cuba signed a peace agreement in New York. On March 21, 1990, Namibia became an independent country.

As head of operations for the Cuban military mission in Angola, I helped plan and organize the withdrawal of our forces. Polo and I returned to Cuba in 1990. The last Cuban internationalist combatants returned home in May 1991.

Internationalist missions in Ethiopia and Mozambique

CALERO: At the same time thousands of Cuban volunteers were aiding Angola, Cuba in 1977 responded to a request for help from the Ethiopian government. The monarchy of Emperor Haile Selassie had been overthrown in 1974. The new government, with ties to Moscow, initiated a land reform that broke the back of feudal relations in Ethiopia and alarmed the imperialist powers.

In July 1977 the government of neighboring Somalia, with US backing, invaded Ethiopia. In response to the Ethiopian government's request, an internationalist mission of some twelve thousand Cuban combatants helped turn the tide. By the opening months of 1978 the Somali invasion had been repelled.

The Ethiopian mission coincided with your first tour in Angola. What were the challenges this simultaneous mission in Africa posed for Cuba?

VILLEGAS: The war in Ethiopia broke out when the Somali government, encouraged by US imperialism, decided to occupy eastern Ethiopia, a vast area known as the Ogaden. They laid territorial claim to it.

In many parts of Africa, the same ethnic population lives on both sides of a border drawn, in most cases, by the imperialist powers. During the decolonization process all the

African states had agreed to maintain the borders inherited from colonial times. Without that agreement Africa could have broken into a thousand countries with one conflict after another.

Cuba previously had advisers in both Somalia and Ethiopia. Our leadership tried to find a political solution to head off the conflict. But the Somali government invaded and Ethiopia asked us to help them militarily. Thousands of Cuban volunteers went to Ethiopia. And we did so without weakening our military commitment to Angola.

Many of our most experienced officers in Angola were sent to Ethiopia. For example, Polo, who had been head of the Cuban military mission and later head of the Southern Front in the first war in Angola, commanded a tank brigade in Ethiopia.

The Ethiopians were good fighters, and our soldiers were well trained. They fought together, and within a few months they expelled the Somali army from Ethiopia. There were relatively few losses.

The situation in Ethiopia posed a number of complexities. There were ethnic conflicts, such as in Eritrea, to the north. The Eritreans didn't identify as Ethiopians and were fighting for their independence.

Cuba favored a political solution to the conflicts involving the different nationalities within Ethiopia. We saw it as an internal problem. We didn't take part in the war between the Ethiopian and Eritrean forces.

At the end of the day, Ethiopia had to recognize the independence of Eritrea and it was established as independent republic. For many years since then we've had doctors and other civilian volunteers working in both Eritrea and Ethiopia.

WATERS: At one point during your mission in Angola, you

“When Somali troops invaded Ethiopia with US backing, the Ethiopian government asked us for military aid. Thousands of Cuban volunteers went to help defend that country. And we did it without weakening our commitment to Angola.”

CIENCIAS SOCIALES

Washington and other imperialist powers were alarmed by the antifeudal land reform initiated by new government after overthrow of Haile Selassie monarchy. In 1977, with imperialist encouragement, Somali troops invaded Ethiopia, occupying Ogaden region. Cuban volunteers joined with Ethiopian soldiers and helped repel the Somali army by March 1978.

Above: Cuban artillery unit in Ethiopia’s Ogaden, February 1978.

went to Mozambique for two months as part of Cuba's internationalist solidarity with that country. What was the objective of that mission?

VILLEGAS: In 1986 or 1987, while I was working in Cuba's special command post for overseas missions, the government of Mozambique asked for help in evaluating the military situation there. Our leadership sent a commission with several specialists, which I headed up.

Under the leadership of FRELIMO, Mozambique won independence from Portugal in 1975, and FRELIMO has since then continued to be the governing party. After independence the governments of Rhodesia and South Africa backed an opposition group, RENAMO (Mozambican National Resistance), which carried out a very destructive war against the new government.

During that war Cuba cooperated with the Mozambican government, sending military advisers and technical specialists. We didn't have troops there as we did in Angola.

CALERO: Mozambique was less economically developed than Angola, wasn't it?

VILLEGAS: In 1975 Mozambique was one of the poorest countries in the world. It had much less mineral wealth than Angola, although it did have coal mines.

The war was having a big impact on the country. RENAMO was not in a position to take power, but they were a strong destabilizing force. They massacred civilians. They disrupted the economy.

When I arrived in Mozambique the two contending forces had reached an impasse. The government didn't have control throughout the country—it mainly held the cities. RENAMO controlled the central region of the country, and government institutions couldn't operate there fully.

During the two months our commission was in Mozambique we traveled across the country, visiting all the military fronts. We reviewed the state of the troops, the military camps, the methods of instruction. What we observed was the absence of any action, the absence of a will to fight.

I met with President Joaquim Chissano and the minister of defense. The defense minister asked me what we recommended to raise people's morale, so the troops would fight and be able to turn around the military situation.

We didn't have any magic wand, I replied. There was no other course than to keep fighting. They had to organize the struggle, carry out ambushes, attack weak points, and constantly and permanently harass the enemy. "You have the magic wand in your own hands: it's called the will to fight and to win," I said.

To do that, it was essential to understand who was the enemy and who wasn't. Because at times the government forces acted as if the entire population was the enemy. That wasn't the case.

Under such conditions of war, the population would accept the authority of whoever had military control of the area. If government troops arrived, they accepted their authority. If RENAMO forces arrived, the population worked with them. People knew how brutal RENAMO was. What they wanted was to live in peace. The people weren't the enemy. It was necessary to win their confidence.

The government's forced conscription policy was one of the problems. Earlier I mentioned that in Angola, UNITA would show up in a town and take the young men with them—they might be fifteen or even twelve. Actually, both sides in Angola did that, although UNITA especially.

The same thing happened in Mozambique during the war. They didn't enlist people on the basis of their consciousness.

The forced conscription of teenagers into armed groups—

and sometimes even children—is a big problem that still exists in much of Africa and some countries in Asia. They take kids away and teach them to shoot. And because of how they are educated, they are sometimes turned into killers.

The war in Mozambique continued until peace accords were signed in 1992. Throughout this time we continued to provide military advisers. The victory in Angola and the end of the apartheid regime gave important breathing room to Mozambique and all neighboring countries.

'Fidel's leadership was decisive'

WATERS: During the final battles that began at Cuito Cuanavale in late 1987, Fidel designated Polo—General Leopoldo Cintra Frías—to lead the southern front, the Southern Troop Grouping (Agrupación de Tropas del Sur, ATS). You worked directly with Polo then, and had worked closely with him at an earlier stage of the Angola mission as well. Polo is today Cuba's minister of the Revolutionary Armed Forces. What kind of leadership did he provide in Angola?

VILLEGAS: At the time of Cuito Cuanavale Polo already had a lot of experience in Angola. He had been one of our first officers to arrive in 1975, serving as head of the Southern Front, which drove out the South African invaders in 1976. As I mentioned before, he was head of the Cuban military mission at the time of the Cangamba battle and afterward.

Polo is a very accessible person. He understood the Angolans well. We had two leaders in Angola who were known for their exceptional ability to connect with people: Polo and Tomassevich. You almost couldn't tell if they were Cuban or Angolan, because they totally identified with the Angolans. The Angolans felt that Polo and Tomassevich were part of them.

Fidel has had a lot of confidence in Polo. Polo comes from a humble background, from a peasant family in the area of the Sierra Maestra mountains in eastern Cuba. He's from Yara, the same town where I was born. Ever since Polo joined the Rebel Army he's shown great military ability. He's an extraordinarily loyal man. Fidel knew that whenever Polo was given a mission, he carried it out to the end. So Fidel assigned him some of the most difficult, complex tasks.

Polo has shown a great aptitude for leadership. I worked with him when he was named head of the military mission in 1983. I was serving as the liaison between the special command post in Havana and the military leadership in Angola.

I described earlier how during the Cangamba battle we had to locate the armored column of reinforcements coming from Menongue and Polo sent me, along with the head of the helicopter unit, to take two helicopters and find the column. As liaison I normally didn't take part in that kind of operation.

"Look, I'm the representative of the high command," I told Polo.

"Man, don't talk to me about the representative of the high command," he replied. "Don't you see? You're one of my brothers, you're from my hometown! Who can I trust more than you?" So I boarded the helicopter.

Later I became head of operations for the Cuban mission and helped plan combat operations. Polo also made me his aide. He'd move around by plane from one place in Angola to another. And if he said, "At 7:00 a.m. we're airborne," we had to be in the plane at 7:00 a.m. He wouldn't wait. Once I arrived running, without even being able to brush my teeth, as he was taking off. "*Negro*, you're staying," he said. That's how it was.

KOPPEL: What about Fidel's leadership of the internationalist campaign in Angola?

"Perhaps you could be asking if it's necessary for a battery of women to go to southern Angola, whether there are no more Cuban men to send over there. The participation of women is not a military necessity. It is a moral necessity, a revolutionary necessity."

—Fidel Castro

Speaking at June 1988 send-off for a battery of the First Women's Antiaircraft Artillery Regiment of Guantánamo, attended by African members of diplomatic corps in Havana

JUVENTUD REBELDE

Above: Lieutenant Milagros Katrina Soto (center) and other members of Women's Antiaircraft Artillery Regiment, which helped defend Angola from attacks by the air force of the apartheid regime.

VILLEGAS: Fidel's leadership was decisive in winning the victory. He was on top of everything, day in and day out. He went to the command post daily.

During the Cangamba battle, Polo spoke to the Commander every day at 7:00 p.m. by radio. I've described the foresight that Fidel demonstrated in that battle and the confidence he inspired in the troops. He was always concerned about the well-being of the combatants.

Che said Fidel's greatness lay in the details. During the struggle in Angola, he wanted to see everything, touch everything, verify everything.

"Don't tell me what Polo or Ochoa told you, or what anyone else told you," he would say to me. "Tell me what you saw and touched yourself. And if it's feasible, bring me some evidence of what you saw and touched." So I got a young soldier from the Interior Ministry with a video camera to go around with me.

As UNITA's actions began escalating and further jeopardized Angola's stability, Fidel followed events even more closely. We had to provide him with more information, and more frequently.

There were days when I flew out of Luanda early in the morning, arrived in Havana around 10:00 p.m., and they'd be waiting for us. You had to come prepared with maps and everything to report to the commander. When we arrived at the Armed Forces Ministry, Fidel would be there for a briefing on the situation. At 6:00 or 7:00 a.m. the next morning I'd be on a flight back.

"This tank, which I ordered removed some time ago, why is it here?" Fidel would ask. "It's very close to the Namibian border, and the South Africans could cross it. Our advisers shouldn't be there."

He'd ask your opinion: "Well, if it were like this, not like

"In response to the attack on Cuito Cuanavale, our leadership decided to assemble a force large enough to deal a decisive defeat to the South Africans."

RICARDO LÓPEZ HEVIA/GRANMA

VERDE OLIVO

In late 1987 South African and UNITA troops attacked FAPLA forces in Cuito Cuanavale, in southeastern Angola. In response, Cuba increased its volunteer forces to more than 50,000 and sent its best pilots and most modern military equipment. The double goal: first, to prevent Cuito Cuanavale from falling and, second, to launch an offensive in southwestern Angola.

Top: Cuban-Angolan tank crew at Cuito Cuanavale, May 31, 1988, after victory was secured.

Bottom: Cuban supply convoy on the way from Menongue to Cuito Cuanavale battlefront.

"Cuito Cuanavale and Calueque were the two main victories that decided the outcome of the war. By August 1988 all South African troops had been pulled out of Angola."

VERDE OLIVO

Top: Cuban anti-aircraft unit that shot down South African Mirage jet, February 1988, during battle of Cuito Cuanavale.

Bottom: In record ten weeks, Cuban workers built airfield at Cahama, near Namibian border. Cuban pilots used airstrip to gain control of skies and threaten South African bases in northern Namibia.

L. GIL/VERDE OLIVO

As South African and UNITA forces were turned back at Cuito Cuanavale, tens of thousands of Cuban and Angolan troops with SWAPO scouts advanced toward Namibian border, shattering invaders' morale. By August 1988 all South African troops had pulled out of Angola. In December, Pretoria signed peace agreement. On March 21, 1990, Namibia became independent nation.

Top: Joint Cuban-SWAPO patrol in southern Angola. Some 2,000 SWAPO combatants were part of drive toward Namibian border.

Bottom: Cuban pilots in southern Angola, April 1988. "The MIG-23s broke our hearts," a demoralized South African soldier wrote on a damaged bridge near Calueque dam.

"Fidel's leadership was decisive to winning the victory in Angola."

Villegas served as liaison between Cuban military mission in Angola and Revolutionary Armed Forces special command post in Havana. "I had to keep the general staff in Havana informed of what was developing," he said. "Fidel was on top of everything day by day."

Top: At Havana special command post, Cuban commander-in-chief Fidel Castro speaks with then Col. Harry Villegas (right), who was reporting to him on battle of Cuito Cuanavale, 1988. On left is Col. Jesús Morejón, head of command post.

Bottom: Villegas (right) with Col. José Toledo (left) and Lt. Col. Nelson González (center) in central Angola during fight against UNITA bands, 1980s.

CIENCIAS SOCIALES

As commander of Cuban forces in Angola, General Leopoldo Cintra Frías, "Polo," was respected by Angola's leadership. "Fidel had a lot of confidence in him," said Villegas. "He assigned Polo some of the most complex missions." **Top:** Cintra Frías (left) talks with Angolan defense minister Pedro Maria Tonha as they coordinate actions during 1983 battle of Cangamba.

The internationalist mission in Angola strengthened Cuban Revolution, "above all in consciousness," Villegas said. This strength was registered in renewal of volunteer work brigades in Cuba that built housing, schools, and other facilities needed by working people. **Bottom:** Volunteer brigade builds child-care center in Havana, late 1980s.

PASTOR BATISTA/GRANMA

Top: January 10, 1989. Luanda residents salute first contingent of Cuban soldiers heading home at end of victorious mission. The last Cuban troops left in May 1991.

Bottom: Mass rally in Namibia celebrates agreement recognizing Namibia's independence from South African rule, December 1988.

ANNA ZIEMINSKI

Defeat of South African army in Angola accelerated mass struggle in South Africa that won freedom of Nelson Mandela and brought down white-supremacist regime.

Top: Rally in Soweto township of Johannesburg, South Africa, celebrates release of African National Congress leader Nelson Mandela, February 11, 1990.

Bottom: Mandela with Cuban president Fidel Castro in Matanzas, Cuba, July 1991. Cuban internationalists in Angola "made a contribution to African independence, freedom, and justice, unparalleled for its principled and selfless character," Mandela said.

"When we face new and unexpected challenges we will always be able to recall the epic of Angola with gratitude, because without Angola we would not be as strong as we are today."

—Raúl Castro, May 1991

Top: Cuban volunteer doctors and nurses, who played decisive role in fighting deadly Ebola outbreak in West Africa, arrive in Freetown, Sierra Leone, and unload their supplies, October 2014.

Bottom: More than a million working people march in Havana on May Day 2015, in a massive show of support for Cuba's socialist revolution. March was led by internationalist medical volunteers who had recently returned from West Africa.

that, what would you do?"

Once, during the battles in Cuito, Fidel asked me, "Do you think the South Africans will attack?"

"No, I don't think they will."

"Are you sure they won't attack?"

"Yes, I'm sure."

"They're going to attack."

So I returned to Angola and I had to tell the head of the mission, "The Commander says they're going to attack, that we have to take certain positions and measures."

Then, when I returned to Havana, Fidel asked me again, "Do you think they're going to attack?"

"Yes, that's what you told me."

"No, they're not going to attack."

And I asked myself, how am I going to return and explain this to the chief of the mission?

Fidel always kept analyzing everything, the changing elements, and drew his conclusions.

Sometimes I made problems for myself. Fidel would walk around and I'd walk right behind him. He'd ask me questions and I answered him. And sometimes he didn't ask me and I'd tell him my opinion anyway. Some of the top officers told me, "Villegas, that shows a lack of respect." They wanted me to report to the commander, stand still, and say nothing more.

That was hard for me. It wasn't a lack of respect. It's that Fidel inspires confidence. He creates a personal connection that makes you feel it's your duty to say what you think. Perhaps others didn't like that. But Fidel did.

WATERS: In mid-1989, after the victory in Angola, General Arnaldo Ochoa and three other officers of Cuba's Revolutionary Armed Forces and Interior Ministry were tried and executed for hostile acts against a foreign state, drug trafficking, and abuse of office.[1] Ochoa had been head of the Cuban military mission in Angola in 1987–88.

Fidel put it this way—in Angola, he said, "at the same time that the most glorious page was being written, the most shameful one was being written, in large measure by the head of the Cuban military mission in Angola."

Advances by the Cuban Revolution in the late 1980s, which included the rectification process in Cuba as well as the victories won in Angola, made it possible for the revolutionary leadership and the people of Cuba to confront that bitter episode. How do you view the significance of those events?

VILLEGAS: When the leadership of the revolution became aware of the situation regarding Ochoa, it immediately investigated the facts and settled the issue. This was done in front of the people of the world and the people of Cuba. It could have instead been investigated and resolved internally. But it was important to make clear how the leadership of the party, the government, and the Revolutionary Armed Forces acted. It was important that nothing was hidden. That those who were responsible for the crimes would be prosecuted and punished. And that's what was done.

The corrupt actions of Ochoa in Angola in and of themselves were of little material importance. He bought some diamonds and tried to sell them on the black market. He was ignorant about diamonds and bought tiny chips, the ones nobody buys and get dumped. But theft and embezzlement of

1. In June–July 1989, Division General Arnaldo Ochoa, a member of the Central Committee of the Communist Party of Cuba; an aide to Ochoa in the FAR; and two Interior Ministry officers were tried, convicted, and executed. Several other army and Interior Ministry officers were convicted and sentenced to prison terms from 10 to 30 years. Trial proceedings were published in the press and broadcast on TV and radio in Cuba.

economic resources are incompatible with socialism.

Ochoa was head of the military mission in Angola. But Polo was named commander of the Southern Front, where the outcome of the war was decided and the victory was won. At that time Ochoa was mainly involved in other responsibilities of the Cuban mission, which had no bearing on the military operations.

Ochoa went to Angola with his record as a Rebel Army combatant, internationalist in Venezuela and Ethiopia, Hero of the Republic. As head of the military mission in Angola he represented the prestige of our revolution.

In the trial, Ochoa's involvement in drug trafficking was proven. His aide, Captain Jorge Martínez, met with Pablo Escobar—head of the Medellín drug cartel—to explore the possibility of using Cuban territory for Escobar's operations. Ochoa admitted all the charges brought against him in the trial.

US imperialism could have used all of that in its campaign of lies, accusing the Cuban government of involvement in drug trafficking.

The response of our revolutionary leadership was an example of honesty, of determination to fight corruption and defend the principles of socialism. It showed the moral strength of the revolution.

WATERS: The internationalist aid to Angola over a nearly sixteen-year period was an enormous effort for a relatively small and economically underdeveloped nation such as Cuba. Beginning in 1989, almost simultaneous with the end of the Angola mission, the disintegration of the Soviet bloc regimes led to the collapse of most of Cuba's foreign trade agreements and many aid projects, sparking the severe economic crisis of the 1990s. Some Cubans express the view that the resources that went to help Angola should have been used at home.

VILLEGAS: Cuba's aid to Angola was not only worthwhile,

With these exemplary measures, the revolution is stronger

What were the circumstances in which the events leading up to the trial of Ochoa took place? We were in the midst of a war in which our country staked everything, sending its best weapons and more than fifty thousand men. . . .

In face of South Africa's escalation at Cuito Cuanavale, we sent Polo as commander of the Southern Front, where the main operations would be conducted. We left Ochoa as head of the mission. . . .

At the same time the most glorious page in our history was being written, the most shameful one was being written, in large measure by the head of the Cuban military mission in Angola. . . .

Our army is characterized by its discipline, its unconditional loyalty to the principles of the revolution and the party. . . . Ochoa impudently placed himself above the law because he was a hero, a general, a member of the Central Committee. If this precedent had gone unpunished in an exemplary way, it would have been disastrous. . . .

Who would ever speak of rectification again when this mockery of the principles of the rectification process was taking place?[2] . . .

[If the maximum sentences are imposed] the rectification process will not suffer; it will benefit. . . . It will be better understood. The party will be in a much stronger position to apply standards, as well as to sweep away all that smells rotten. . . .

> What do the lives of these gentlemen [Ochoa and others convicted] have in common with the life of a worker? . . . They are two different worlds. And we cannot rest until here there is one single world. Not the world of the bourgeoisie or the petty bourgeoisie, but the world of our workers, our working class, our farmers.
>
> FIDEL CASTRO
> REMARKS AT MEETING OF CUBA'S COUNCIL OF STATE
> JULY 9, 1989

but if we were in a position to do it again, we would.

If the South African army had not been defeated in Angola, would apartheid have been eliminated when it was? If we did nothing more than indirectly help defeat apartheid, our effort was unquestionably worthwhile.

Thanks to the victory in Angola, the Namibian people won their independence.

Perhaps it was a dream of ours to think that socialism could be built in Angola. But South Africa was prevented from carving up and dominating Angola.

Whether or not the final objectives were achieved, these are glorious pages in the history of the peoples that have created the foundations for the future.

The internationalist mission in Angola strengthened us in every respect. But above all, I would say, in consciousness.

Angola exposed us to a reality very different from what we were familiar with in Cuba. We lived and struggled together with the Angolan people. We saw with our own eyes the legacy of centuries of colonialism and imperialism in Af-

2. See glossary, Rectification process.

"Angola is an honorable page in the history of solidarity among peoples, of internationalism, of Cuba's contribution to the cause of freedom and human progress."

—Raúl Castro
May 27, 1991

JORGE OLLER/GRANMA

ORLANDO CARDONA/GRANMA

Top: Havana, January 10, 1989: Raúl Castro, minister of Cuba's Revolutionary Armed Forces, greets one of first contingents withdrawn from Angola after signing of December 1988 accords.

Bottom: Raúl Castro speaks at Havana ceremony welcoming home final group of Cuban volunteers, May 27, 1991.

Thanks to Angola, we know better what we are capable of achieving

When we face new and unexpected challenges we will always be able to recall the epic of Angola with gratitude, because without Angola we would not be as strong as we are today.

If our people know themselves better, if all of us know much better what we are capable of achieving—veterans as well as our young people, the new generations—that, too, is thanks to Angola. . . .

Thanks to Angola, we understand in all its dimensions Comrade Fidel's point that when a people like the Cuban people have been capable of fighting and making sacrifices for the freedom of another people, what wouldn't they be capable of doing for themselves.

If today we are more mature in our reflections and decisions, if today we are more staunch, more experienced, that too is thanks to Angola.

If today we are more aware of the work of the revolution, because we have experienced the disastrous remnants of neocolonialism and underdevelopment, for that we must thank Angola. . . .

If our people are now prepared to confront any difficulty in the times ahead, if they're confident about themselves and their ability to resist, to continue developing the country, and to succeed, that confidence reflects our experience of how we grew in the face of adversity and won in Angola.

RAÚL CASTRO
MAY 27, 1991

rica: hunger, disease, illiteracy, deep inequalities. The consequences of a system of exploitation that doesn't value the life of ordinary people.

That experience enriched us. It allowed us to better understand everything we have achieved with the revolution. To understand that the values of the revolution are superior to those of capitalism, where "every man for himself" prevails.

Hundreds of thousands of Cubans proved capable of self-sacrifice, of acting on behalf of other human beings, of defending sister peoples against the apartheid regime.

All that strengthened us politically.

The generations that went through those experiences included three of our Five Heroes—Gerardo, Fernando, and René—who later carried out an internationalist mission in the United States in defense of the revolution.[3]

It was not only a learning experience for those who took part in the internationalist mission. When you know that your father or mother or grandfather went to Angola as a volunteer, thousands of kilometers away, without receiving a cent, and risked his or her life, you admire and learn from that example.

As Raúl said, thanks to Angola, "all of us know much better what we are capable of achieving." In the 1990s the experience of Angola helped us survive the hard years of the Special Period.

Today in Cuba we face big economic challenges. Without economic progress there can be no socialism. Our goal is to increase production of the means of subsistence, and to do it more efficiently. But above all else, we have to put human beings at the center of everything we do.

That's what we did in Angola. We proved capable of giving

3. See glossary: Cuban Five.

all in exchange for nothing. Nothing but the satisfaction of having fulfilled our commitment to humanity.

That's very important for the education of the new generations.

What Raúl said when our combatants returned from Angola in 1991 remains true today: "When we face new and unexpected challenges we will always be able to recall the epic of Angola with gratitude, because without Angola we would not be as strong as we are today."

Chronology

1959

January 1 — Rebel Army under Fidel Castro's command accepts surrender in Santiago de Cuba by forces of US-backed Batista dictatorship. Working people respond to Rebel Army call for island-wide insurrection and general strike.

January 8 — Castro arrives in Havana, culminating Rebel Army "Freedom Caravan," stopping at towns along way as insurrection spreads, explaining revolution's goals and mobilizing participation by workers and farmers.

May 17 — First agrarian reform law. Peasants and workers mobilize, confiscate land above 1,000 acres of Cuban, US, and other foreign owners. Titles distributed to 100,000 landless peasants. Washington responds with mounting attacks.

1960

August–October — In face of escalating US aggression, workers backed by revolutionary government expropriate Cuban, US, and other foreign-owned banks and enterprises.

1961

January — Patrice Lumumba, prime minister of Congo (Zaire), which won independence from Belgium in 1960, is murdered by US- and Belgian-backed Congolese forces.

January — Washington breaks diplomatic relations with Cuba.)

April — US organizes invasion of Cuba's southern coast by 1,500

Cuban mercenaries at Bay of Pigs. They are rapidly defeated by Cuba's revolutionary militias, armed forces, and police at Playa Girón. Fidel Castro is at front with victorious defense forces.

December — Cuba sends arms to aid Algerian independence struggle from France and provides medical care and refuge in Cuba to war-wounded fighters and orphans.

1962

February — Washington imposes total embargo on trade and other commercial and financial ties with Cuba, building on more than two years of economic warfare.

October 22–28 — Mass mobilizations of Cuban workers and farmers stay US invasion plans, after White House brings world to brink of nuclear conflict in "missile crisis."

1963

April–May — Black rights fighters in Birmingham, Alabama, conduct marches and combat cop assaults. "Battle of Birmingham" is turning point in proletarian-led movement that in 1964–65 wins voting rights and other laws striking down "Jim Crow" segregation in US South.

May — Algeria, which won eight-year independence war in July 1962, receives 55 Cuban doctors, dentists, and nurses, Cuba's first internationalist medical mission.

October — Nearly 700 Cuban volunteer combatants help defend Algeria from US-backed Moroccan invasion.

1964

August — Washington fakes naval shelling incident at Gulf of Tonkin in Vietnam as pretext to escalate US war against liberation struggle. US troops increase from 23,000 to 540,000 by 1968.

1965

January — Che Guevara meets with MPLA leader Agostinho Neto in Congo-Brazzaville. Agrees to provide Cuban instructors to train Angolan independence fighters.

April–November — Column of 128 Cuban volunteers, under Guevara's leadership, joins Lumumba supporters in eastern Congo (Zaire) fighting proimperialist Mobutu regime, which is aided by CIA and South African, Belgian, and other mercenaries.

1965–1967

Cuban unit in Congo-Brazzaville, led by Jorge Risquet and Rolando Kindelán, trains MPLA guerrillas and helps defend Congo-Brazzaville government against threats from Mobutu.

1966–1974

Cuban instructors train combatants of PAIGC, led by Amilcar Cabral, fighting for independence of Guinea-Bissau and Cape Verde from Portuguese rule.

1974

April 25 — Military coup in Portugal overthrows decaying fascist dictatorship, unleashing upsurge known as "Carnation Revolution." Key factor in regime's fall is advance of struggles against Portuguese rule in Africa.

September 10 — Guinea-Bissau wins independence from Portugal. Luís Cabral of PAIGC becomes first president. Cape Verde independence proclaimed following year.

September 12 — Monarchy of Emperor Haile Selassie is overthrown. Land reform and other anti-feudal measures spur mobilizations by peasants, workers, and youth, alarming imperialist powers.

1975

January 15 — Alvor Agreement is signed by Portuguese government, MPLA, FNLA, and UNITA; sets Angola's independence for November 11, 1976.

March — FNLA attacks MPLA centers in Luanda but is driven from city after four months of clashes.

April 30 — As US forces abandon Saigon (Ho Chi Minh City) in massive helicopter airlift, Vietnamese fighters win decades-long battle for liberation and national reunification.

June 25 — Mozambique independence from Portugal declared. Samora Machel of FRELIMO, which led independence struggle, becomes president.

July — Washington begins covert military aid to FNLA, UNITA.

August–October — In response to MPLA request, Cuba sends 480 military instructors to train new Angolan army. Cuban volunteers set up four training centers.

October 14 — South African troops invade Angola from south, moving rapidly toward Luanda. US-backed FNLA and Zairean troops advance on Luanda from north.

November 7 — In response to Angolan request for combat forces, Cuban government launches Operation Carlota. Cuba sends by plane initial battalion of 650 Ministry of Interior special forces.

November 8–12 — FAPLA troops and Cuban instructors rout Zairean invasion of Cabinda, the center of Angola's oil industry.

November 10 — FAPLA troops and Cuban volunteers defeat FNLA-Zairean forces at Quifangondo, 15 miles north of Luanda.

November 11 — Angola declares independence. MPLA leader Agostinho Neto is first president.

December 1975–March 1976 — FAPLA-Cuban counteroffensive, led by Cuban commander Víctor Schueg, takes FNLA and Zairean strongholds in north, drives invaders back into Zaire. Cuban troops block South African troops in central Angola, pushing them south. Thousands more combatants arrive from Cuba, reaching 36,000.

1976

March 27 — Last South African troops retreat from Angola.

March — FAPLA, aided by Cuban advisers, begins eliminating remnants of FNLA forces in north and launches fight against UNITA bands in central and southern Angola. Over following three years, UNITA suffers major blows.

June 16 — Police fire on protesting schoolchildren in Soweto, South Africa, killing more than 600, sparking nationwide protests against apartheid and growing world anti-apartheid movement.

1977

March 8 — Zairean exiles, based in Angola, cross into Zaire, trying to spark secessionist uprising in Katanga province. Mobutu regime, aided by Moroccan troops, drives them back into Angola.

Late March — Cuban president Fidel Castro visits Angola. Affirms that Cuba will defend Angola against South African intervention, urges FAPLA to focus on fighting UNITA.

May 27 — Coup against Neto government, led by Nito Alves, is defeated. Cuban forces help defend government.

November — 12,000-strong Cuban internationalist mission helps defend Ethiopia from US-backed Somali army invasion, which is defeated by March 1978.

1978

May 4 — South African forces attack UN-supported Namibian refugee camp in Cassinga, southern Angola. Some 600 massacred. Hundreds of surviving children are brought to Cuba for medical care and schooling.

1979

January — With improved military situation, Cuba withdraws advisers from FAPLA units fighting UNITA. Cuban troops pull back from area near Namibian border and form defensive line some 250 kilometers north to block South African invasions.

February 11 — After year of mobilizations in Iran by workers, peasants, and youth, insurrection topples monarchy of the shah, who had fled in mid-January.

March 13 — Led by Maurice Bishop, working people in east Caribbean island of Grenada overturn US-backed dictatorship and establish revolutionary government. Over next four and a half years, Cuban internationalists volunteer there as construction workers, teachers, and medical personnel.

July 19 — Popular insurrection in Nicaragua, led by Sandinista National Liberation Front, overturns Somoza dictatorship. In 1980s, as Washington organizes counterrevolutionary ("contra") war against FSLN-led government, Cuba sends thousands of volunteer teachers, doctors, and technicians.

September 10 — Agostinho Neto dies. José Eduardo dos Santos becomes president.

1980

June — South Africa targets SWAPO in major raid into southwestern Angola. In following years, Pretoria steps up attacks in south and UNITA gains strength.

1981

January — In response to growing US military threats and activity in Central America and Caribbean, Cuba declares defense strategy of War of the Entire People and establishes volunteer Territorial Troop Militias.

May — Angolan government asks Cuba to resume providing advisers in fight against UNITA. Under *Operación Olivo,* commanded by Cuban general Raúl Menéndez Tomassevich, Cuban advisers are assigned to FAPLA light infantry brigades for irregular warfare against UNITA.

August — More than four thousand South African troops invade southwest Angola, occupying much of Cunene province.

1983

August 2–14 — South African-officered UNITA troops attack isolated southeastern town of Cangamba. With Cuban air support, outnumbered Cuban and Angolan forces resist week-long siege.

October 19 — Grenada's revolutionary government overthrown. Maurice Bishop and other leaders are assassinated. Counterrevolution opens road to US invasion a week later.

1984

March 25 — 300 Angolan militia members and 230 Cuban civilian volunteers repel attack by 1,500 UNITA troops on Sumbe on Angola's west central coast.

September — Black townships in South Africa explode in wave of strikes, demonstrations, and school boycotts that continue over next year. International support grows.

1985

August–September — At urging of Soviet advisers, FAPLA

launches offensive against UNITA in Mavinga, a southeastern town far from reinforcements and supply points. South African forces inflict heavy casualties.

August 26 — Chernobyl nuclear disaster in Ukraine leads to cancer and other radiation-caused disease among tens of thousands. Cuba offers medical aid, eventually bringing 25,000 children to Cuba for treatment and rehabilitation.

October — Meeting in Cuba with Soviet foreign minister, Fidel insists it's time to "cut off the hands" of apartheid regime inside Angola.

1986

April — Fidel Castro announces rectification process, turning away from more than a decade of copying bureaucratic Soviet economic and management policies stifling workers' initiative. Cubans launch voluntary work brigades to build child-care centers, schools, clinics, housing. Social movement expands until economic crisis of Special Period in early 1990s dries up material resources.

September 2 — "We are willing to keep our soldiers in Angola as long as apartheid exists," Fidel Castrol says at Nonaligned summit in Harare, Zimbabwe.

November — Iran-Contra scandal exposes secret US arms sales to Iran and covert funding of counterrevolutionaries fighting to overturn FSLN-led government in Nicaragua.

1987

September–October — After failed FAPLA offensive in southeast, Angolan troops take heavy casualties at South Africa's hands and are pursued to town of Cuito Cuanavale.

November 15 — Cuban leadership resolves to send resources necessary to drive South African forces from Angola. Troop strength is boosted from 38,000 to 55,000 by August 1988.

December — First Cuban troops join defense of Cuito Cuanavale. Cuban MIGS and antiaircraft artillery gain control of airspace over southern Angola for first time.

1988

January 29 — US officials for first time agree to Cuban participation in ongoing Angolan-South African-US talks. Washington insists Cuban troops leave Angola before South Africa withdraws.

March 23 — Angolan and Cuban combatants turn back last major South African assault on Cuito Cuanavale.

Late March — Tens of thousands of Cuban, FAPLA, and SWAPO combatants advance south toward Namibian border.

May 4 — Mass rallies in Namibian towns on 10th anniversary of Cassinga massacre defy cops' rubber bullets and tear gas.

Mid-May — In counteroffensive, 10,000 Cuban, 7,000 FAPLA, and 2,000 SWAPO troops, deploying 200 tanks, come within 20 miles of Namibian border.

Early June — Cuban construction workers complete airstrip, begun ten weeks earlier, in Cahama, 40 miles from Namibia border. Cuban jet fighters begin flying over northern Namibia, near South African air bases.

June 26–27 — In response to Pretoria's attack on Cuban patrol at Tchipa, Cuban MIGS strafe South African unit at Calueque dam near Namibian border. South Africans retreat into Namibia.

July 22 — At talks in Cape Verde, Cuban representatives offer to halt advance to Namibia if Pretoria's troops leave Angola within three weeks. South Africans capitulate.

August 30 — Last South African soldiers leave Angola.

December 22 — South African-Angolan-Cuban accord signed

at United Nations in New York; terms set withdrawal of South African and Cuban troops, as well as Namibia's independence from Pretoria.

1989

January — First units of Cuban troops withdraw from Angola.

November 7–11 — SWAPO wins first free elections in Namibia.

1990

February — In face of rising mass struggle in South Africa, Nelson Mandela, leader of African National Congress (ANC), walks free from prison after 27 years. Pretoria lifts ban on ANC and other organizations.

March 21 — Namibia declares independence, with SWAPO leader Sam Nujoma elected president.

1991

May 25 — Last Cuban troops return home from Angola.

July 26 — Nelson Mandela speaks in Cuba, thanking internationalist volunteers for their "unparalleled contribution to African independence."

1992

September 29–30 — MPLA defeats UNITA in Angolan elections. UNITA rejects results, resumes fighting; war continues until 2002, when UNITA leader Jonas Savimbi is killed in battle.

1994

April 27 — Nelson Mandela is elected president of South Africa in first post-apartheid election.

Glossary of individuals, organizations, and events

Acevedo, Enrique (1942–) – Brigadier general in Cuba's Revolutionary Armed Forces. Rebel Army combatant in Che Guevara's column that crossed Cuba from Sierra Maestra mountains to the Escambray. Commanded Mechanized Infantry Regiment in Angola 1977–79; returned to Angola 1987–89.

Alves, Nito (1945–1977) – Interior minister in Angolan government after independence in 1975. Headed faction in MPLA opposed to Neto leadership. Led failed 1977 coup; arrested and executed after its defeat.

Alvor Agreement – See chronology, January 15, 1975.

Apartheid – State structure in South Africa based on white-supremacist racial caste system, disenfranchising big majority of population. Overturned by mass struggle from mid-1970s through early '90s, culminating in 1994 with election of African National Congress leader Nelson Mandela as president of South Africa.

Batista, Fulgencio (1901–1973) – Military strongman in Cuba 1934–58. Led 1952 coup establishing dictatorship backed by Washington. Fled Cuba January 1, 1959, in face of advancing Rebel Army, popular insurrection, and general strike.

Bay of Pigs – See chronology, April 1961.

Cabral, Amilcar (1924–1973) – Founding leader in 1956 of African Party for the Independence of Guinea and Cape Verde

(PAIGC). Led guerrilla war from 1963 that won independence for Guinea-Bissau 1974 and Cape Verde 1975. Assassinated January 1973.

Caetano, Marcelo (1906–80) – Portuguese dictator, toppled April 1974 in military coup that sparked mass popular uprising known as "Carnation Revolution."

Carlota – A slave in Matanzas, Cuba, who led 1843 slave rebellion against Spanish colonial government. Captured and killed as revolt was crushed. Cuba's 1975–91 combat mission in Angola was named "Operation Carlota."

Carnation Revolution – See chronology, April 25, 1974.

Cassinga – See chronology, May 4, 1978.

Castro, Fidel (1926–2016) – Central leader of revolutionary movement in Cuba since outset of struggle against Batista dictatorship in 1952. Organized July 26, 1953, armed assault on Moncada garrison in Santiago de Cuba and garrison in Bayamo. Led fusion of revolutionaries to found July 26 Revolutionary Movement. Organized *Granma* expedition from Mexico to launch revolutionary war in Cuba 1956. Commander in chief Rebel Army 1956–59; commander in chief Revolutionary Armed Forces 1959–2008. Cuba's prime minister, then president of Council of State and Council of Ministers 1959–2008. First secretary Communist Party of Cuba 1965–2011.

Castro, Raúl (1931–) – President of Cuba's Council of State and Council of Ministers since 2008; first secretary of Communist Party of Cuba since 2011. Participated in 1953 attack on Moncada barracks. Founding member July 26 Movement and participant in *Granma* expedition. Rebel Army commander of Second Eastern Front 1958. General of the Army; Minister of Revolutionary Armed Forces 1959–2008.

Chissano, Joaquim (1939–) – FRELIMO leader; second president of Mozambique 1986–2005.

Cintra Frías, Leopoldo (Polo) (1941–) – Army corps general; since 2011 minister of Cuba's Revolutionary Armed Forces, member Council of State. Rebel Army combatant in Sierra Maestra Column 1 under Fidel Castro's command. Commanded forces on Angola's Southern Front 1975–76. Internationalist mission in Ethiopia 1978. Headed Cuba's military mission in Angola 1983–86 and 1989. Hero of the Republic of Cuba.

Congo-Brazzaville (formally Republic of the Congo) – Won independence from France 1960.

Congo, Democratic Republic of – Won independence from Belgium 1960. Officially named Zaire 1971–97.

Cuban Five – In 1990s Gerardo Hernández, Ramón Labañino, Antonio Guerrero, Fernando González, and René González, who became known as the Cuban Five, took assignments reporting to Cuban government on counterrevolutionary groups in US planning attacks on Cuba. Arrested in Miami and framed by US government in 1998 on "espionage conspiracy" and other charges, they spent 13 to 16 years in federal prisons. Three served as volunteer combatants in Angola: René González (1977–79), Fernando González (1987–89), and Gerardo Hernández (1989–90).

Díaz Argüelles, Raúl (1936–1975) – First head of Cuba's internationalist mission in Angola; killed by land mine December 1975. Commander in Rebel Army in Escambray mountains. In early 1970s oversaw Cuban assistance to anti-imperialist movements in Latin America and Africa. Posthumously promoted to brigadier general. Hero of the Republic of Cuba.

Dos Santos, José Eduardo (1942–) – President of Angola since 1979, following death of first president, Agostinho Neto. Joined MPLA 1956. Foreign minister after independence.

Dreke, Víctor (1937–) – Second in command, under Che Guevara, of Cuban column in Congo 1965. Led Cuban internationalists aiding Guinea-Bissau independence fighters 1966–68. Revolutionary Directorate and Rebel Army combatant in Escambray; in 1960–65 led forces in Escambray that defeated US-backed counterrevolutionary bands. President of Cuba-Africa Friendship Association and of Association of Combatants of the Cuban Revolution in Havana Province.

Espinosa Martín, Ramón (1939–) – Army corps general. Since 2009 vice minister of Cuba's Revolutionary Armed Forces. Revolutionary Directorate and Rebel Army combatant in Escambray mountains. Led Cuban forces in Cabinda, Angola, 1975–76. Head of Cuban military mission in Ethiopia 1980–82. Hero of the Republic of Cuba.

FAPLA (People's Armed Forces for the Liberation of Angola) – Originating as MPLA's armed wing in fight against Portuguese colonialism, became Angola's armed forces after independence in 1975.

FNLA (National Front for the Liberation of Angola) – Formed 1962, led by Holden Roberto. One of armed groups fighting Portuguese colonialism in Angola. Waged war against MPLA-led government at time of independence in 1975, with backing of Mobutu regime in Zaire and US government. Largely defeated in 1976.

FRELIMO (Mozambique Liberation Front) – Founded 1962, led Mozambique independence struggle. First two presidents were Eduardo Mondlane and Samora Machel. Governing party since Mozambique's independence in 1975.

Girón – See chronology, April 1961.

Guevara, Ernesto Che (1928–1967) – Born in Argentina, became a central leader of Cuban Revolution. Joined *Granma* expedition in Mexico as troop doctor; became Rebel Army commander July 1957. Headed National Bank, Ministry of

Industry, held other leading responsibilities in revolutionary government. Led Cuban volunteer combat mission in eastern Congo 1965. Went to Bolivia 1966 to lead guerrilla movement against military dictatorship there. Wounded, captured, and killed October 1967 by Bolivian army in CIA-directed operation.

Iran-Contra scandal – See chronology, November 1986.

Kindelán, Roberto (1928–2016) – Brigadier general in Cuba's Revolutionary Armed Forces. Rebel Army combatant in Che Guevara's column in Sierra Maestra mountains crossing Cuba to Escambray mountains. Military commander of Cuban volunteers in Congo-Brazzaville to help defend government of country newly independent from France and train MPLA Angolan independence fighters 1965–67.

Kurochkin, Konstantin – Lieutenant-general, head of Soviet military mission in Angola 1982–85.

Lara, Lúcio (1929–2016) – Founding member MPLA and longtime Central Committee member. MPLA organization secretary during Angolan civil war.

Mandela, Nelson (1918–2013) – Led African National Congress in anti-apartheid struggle in South Africa from mid-1940s. Arrested 1962, imprisoned until 1990. Released amid growing mass struggle against white supremacist regime, given major boost by 1988 defeat of apartheid army in Angola. Elected president of South Africa 1994 in first post-apartheid election, serving until 1999.

Menéndez Tomassevich, Raúl (1929–2001) – Headed Cuban military mission in Angola 1977–79, 1981–83. Commanded Rebel Army column in Second Eastern Front led by Raúl Castro. Commanded special forces fighting counterrevolutionary bandits in central Cuba 1961–63. Internationalist missions in Guinea-Bissau 1966, Venezuela 1967. Hero of the Republic of Cuba. Division general at time of death.

Mobutu Sese Seko (1930–1997) – Army chief of staff in Congo after independence; led 1960 Belgian- and US-organized coup against first prime minister Patrice Lumumba. Proclaimed himself president 1965, holding power with Washington's backing until overthrown 1997.

Moncada attack – On July 26, 1953, 160 combatants under command of Fidel Castro launched insurrectionary attacks on Moncada army garrison in Santiago de Cuba and in Bayamo, opening revolutionary struggle against Batista dictatorship. Attack failed. Most of those captured were massacred. Broad amnesty campaign won release May 1955 of others rounded up and imprisoned, including Fidel Castro and Raúl Castro.

Moracén Limonta, Rafael (1939–) – Brigadier general in Cuba's Revolutionary Armed Forces. Rebel Army combatant in Third Eastern Front under Juan Almeida's command. In Congo-Brazzaville 1965–67, led Cuban volunteers training MPLA fighters for Angolan independence. Headed tank brigade in Cabinda, then head of Cuban advisers to presidential guard for Agostinho Neto 1975-82. Hero of the Republic of Cuba.

MPLA (Popular Movement for the Liberation of Angola) – Founded 1956, waged guerrilla struggle for Angola's independence from Portugal. From 1962 led by Agostinho Neto. Following independence in 1975 became governing party.

Neto, Agostinho (1922–1979) – Leader of fight against Portuguese rule in Angola. MPLA president from 1962; jailed, exiled for anticolonial activity. President of Angola 1975 until his death.

Ochoa, Arnaldo (1940–1989) – Former division general. While heading Cuba's Angola mission 1987–88, instigated blackmarketeering and smuggling of ivory, diamonds to fund operations; organized subordinates to meet with Medellín drug cartel. In 1989 he and three other high-ranking officers of Revolutionary Armed Forces and Ministry of Interior were tried, convicted, and executed.

PAIGC (African Party for the Independence of Guinea and Cape Verde) – Led by Amilcar Cabral, took up arms against Portuguese rule in 1963. Won Guinea-Bissau independence 1974, Cape Verde 1975.

Playa Girón – See chronology, April 1961.

Portuguese revolution – See chronology, April 25, 1974.

Rectification process – See chronology, April 1986.

RENAMO (Mozambican National Resistance) – Group backed by white-supremacist regimes in Rhodesia and South Africa in post-independence war to overthrow FRELIMO government in Mozambique. War lasted from 1977 to early 1990s. Remains main opposition party.

Risquet Valdés, Jorge (1930–2016) – Led Cuban volunteers in Congo-Brazzaville helping defend government against pro-imperialist forces and train MPLA Angolan independence fighters 1965–66. Youth leader of Popular Socialist Party; Rebel Army combatant in Second Eastern Front under Raúl Castro's command. Headed Cuba's civilian mission in Angola 1975–79. Cuba's chief negotiator in 1988 talks that ended South African intervention.

Roberto, Holden (1923–2007) – Led faction of Angola's independence fight from 1956. FNLA founding leader 1962. Worked with CIA and Mobutu dictatorship in Zaire to topple MPLA-led government.

Savimbi, Jonas (1934–2002) – Led faction of Angola's independence fight from 1960. UNITA founding leader 1966. Allied with Pretoria and Washington 1975 to overturn MPLA-led government. After defeat of South African intervention, continued war against Luanda. Killed in battle, leading to ceasefire in 27-year war.

Schueg Colás, Víctor (1936–1998) – Brigadier general in Cuba's Revolutionary Armed Forces. Rebel Army combatant in Second Eastern Front led by Raúl Castro. Part of Guevara's column during Congo mission 1965. Chief of staff, military mission in Angola 1975–76.

Sékou Touré, Ahmed (1922–1984) – Leader of independence struggle from France in what is today Republic of Guinea (Guinea-Conakry). President from independence in 1958 until his death.

Special Period – Term in Cuba for severe economic conditions in 1990s and revolutionary government's course to address them. With end of USSR and allied Eastern European regimes, Cuba lost 85 percent of its foreign trade, made worse by world capitalist crisis and stepped-up US economic warfare. By 1996 efforts by Cuban working people and government began to revive farm and industrial output, though far below pre-1990 levels, resulting in shortages of food and other essentials.

SWAPO (South West Africa People's Organisation) – Formed 1960, led fight for Namibia's independence from South Africa; founding leader was Sam Nujoma. Fought alongside Cuban-Angolan forces on southern front. Governing party in Namibia since independence in 1990.

Tomassevich, Raúl – See Menéndez Tomassevich, Raúl.

UNITA (National Union for the Total Independence of Angola) – Founded 1966 to fight Portuguese rule, led by Jonas Savimbi. In 1975 allied with apartheid South Africa and Washington to overthrow MPLA-led government of newly independent Angola. For 27 years waged war against Luanda. Signed cease-fire in 2002, after Savimbi was killed in battle.

Index

Also by Harry Villegas "Pombo"

Pombo: A Man of Che's *guerrilla*

With Che Guevara in Bolivia, 1966–68

A diary and account of the guerrilla campaign in Bolivia led by Ernesto Che Guevara. The author, a member of Che's general staff there and later a brigadier general in Cuba's Revolutionary Armed Forces, commanded five surviving guerrillas who eluded encirclement by the Bolivian army and US intelligence forces for more than four months. $25. Also in Spanish.

At the Side of Che Guevara

In two interviews Villegas talks about struggles he took part in over four decades, including the 16-year internationalist mission in Angola that defeated the South African army. He describes fighting alongside anti-imperialist forces in the Congo in 1965; serving in Guevara's column during Cuba's revolutionary war; and helping establish revolutionary Cuba's first military school.
$5. Also in Spanish.

Making History

Interviews with four generals of Cuba's Revolutionary Armed Forces

Che taught me that "the struggle itself reveals who is willing and able to be a leader, and who is not," says Villegas in one of the four interviews here. "The struggle sifts out its own leaders." Four generals recount lessons of the revolutionary war in Cuba.
$17. Also in Spanish and Farsi.

Cuba's internationalist

Cuba and Angola

Fighting for Africa's Freedom and Our Own

FIDEL CASTRO, RAÚL CASTRO, NELSON MANDELA, GABRIEL GARCÍA MÁRQUEZ

In March 1988, the army of South Africa's apartheid regime was dealt a crushing defeat by Cuban, Angolan, and Namibian combatants in Angola. Here leaders and participants tell the story of the 16- year-long internationalist mission that strengthened the Cuban Revolution as well.

$12. Also in Spanish.

How Far We Slaves Have Come!

South Africa and Cuba in Today's World

NELSON MANDEL, FIDEL CASTRO

Speaking together in Cuba in 1991, Mandela and Castro discuss the place in the history of Africa of the victory by Cuban, Angolan, and Namibian combatants over the US-backed South African army that had invaded Angola. Cuba's internationalist volunteers, said Mandela, made an "unparalleled contribution to African independence, freedom, and justice."

$10. Also in Spanish and Farsi.

From the Escambray to the Congo

In the Whirlwind of the Cuban Revolution

VÍCTOR DREKE

A leading participant in Cuba's revolutionary movement for more than half a century describes his experiences as second-in-command in the 1965 internationalist mission in Congo led by Che Guevara. He describes the creative joy of working people in Cuba, at home and abroad, as they've defended their revolutionary course.

$18. Also in Spanish.

missions worldwide

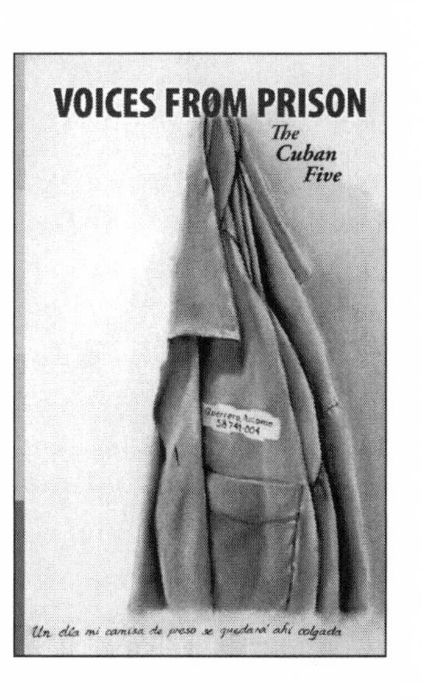

Voices from Prison

The Cuban Five

Cuban internationalists Gerardo Hernández, Ramón Labañino, Antonio Guerrero, Fernando González, and René González, known to millions worldwide as the Cuban Five, were framed up and imprisoned by Washington for up to 16 years. In the voices heard here from fellow prisoners, freedom fighters, and family members their revolutionary integrity, humanity—and humor—emerge ever more clearly.

$7. Also in Spanish, French, Farsi, and Arabic.

In Defense of Socialism

Four Speeches on the 30th Anniversary of the Cuban Revolution, 1988–89

FIDEL CASTRO

Castro describes the decisive place of volunteer Cuban fighters in the final stage of the war in Angola against invading forces of South Africa's apartheid regime. Not only is economic and social progress possible without capitalism's dog-eat-dog competition, the Cuban leader says, but socialism is humanity's only way forward.

$15 Also in Greek.

Bolivian Diary of Ernesto Che Guevara

Guevara's day-by-day chronicle of the 1966–67 guerrilla campaign in Bolivia, an effort to forge a continent-wide revolutionary movement of workers and peasants and open the road to socialist revolution in South America.

$25. Also in Spanish.

WWW.PATHFINDERPRESS.COM

The US rulers have begun

Three books for today's spreading and deepening debate among working people looking for a way forward in face of capitalism's global economic and social calamity and wars.

The Clintons' Anti-Working-Class Record

Why Washington Fears Working People

Jack Barnes

Hillary Clinton contemptuously called workers who refused to vote for her irredeemable "deplorables."

Winner Donald Trump tries to divide and weaken the working class—demagogically targeting Mexicans, Muslims, unionists, women, and others—while lining the bosses' pockets.

This book documents the profit-driven course over the last quarter century of the party of capital, Democrat and Republican alike. It explains the awakening anger and wide-ranging discussion among working people seeking to understand and resist the capitalists' assaults.

$10. Also in Spanish.

Are They Rich Because They're Smart?

Class, Privilege, and Learning under Capitalism

Jack Barnes

Barnes explains the sharpening class inequalities in the US and takes apart self-serving rationalizations by layers of well-paid professionals that their intelligence and schooling equip them to "regulate" the lives of working people who know our own best interests.

$10. Also in Spanish, French, and Farsi.

Is Socialist Revolution in the US Possible?

A Necessary Debate Among Working People

Mary-Alice Waters

An unhesitating "Yes"—that's the answer by Waters. Possible—but not inevitable. That depends on us. Fighting for a society only working people can create, it's our own capacities we will discover as we cast off the false image of ourselves promoted by those who profit from the exploitation of our labor.

$10. Also in Spanish.

Also from Pathfinder

Malcolm X, Black Liberation, and the Road to Workers Power
Jack Barnes

"Don't start with Blacks as an oppressed nationality. Start with the vanguard place of workers who are Black in broad proletarian-led struggles in the United States. The record is mind-boggling. It's the strength and resilience, not the oppression, that bowls you over." —*Jack Barnes*
$20. Also in Spanish, French, Farsi, Arabic, and Greek.

The Communist Manifesto
Karl Marx and Frederick Engels

Why communism is not a set of preconceived principles but the line of march of the working class toward power, "springing from an existing class struggle, a historical movement going on under our very eyes." The founding document of the modern revolutionary workers movement.
$5. Also in Spanish, French, Farsi, and Arabic.

We Are Heirs of the World's Revolutions
Speeches from the Burkina Faso Revolution 1983–87
Thomas Sankara

How peasants and workers in this West African country established a popular revolutionary government and began to fight hunger, illiteracy, and economic backwardness imposed by imperialist domination. They set an example not only for workers and small farmers in Africa, but their class brothers and sisters the world over.
$10. Also in Spanish, French, and Farsi.

U.S. Imperialism Has Lost the Cold War
Jack Barnes

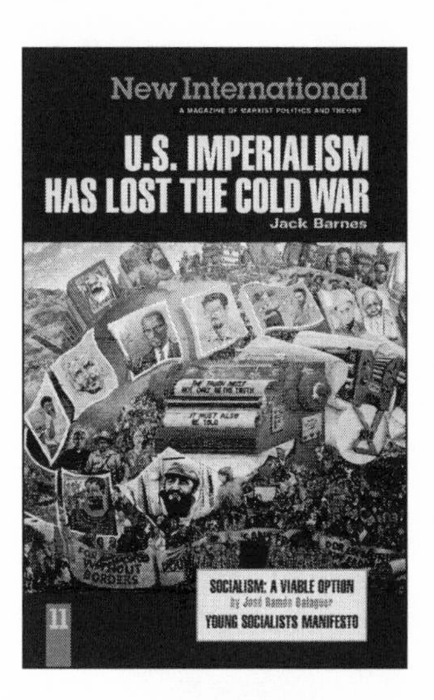

Contrary to imperialist expectations with the collapse of regimes claiming to be communist across Eastern Europe and the USSR, the Cuban Revolution did not follow suit. Cuban working people and their leadership have continued to show the world what "socialist revolution" means. In *New International* no. 11. $16. Also in Spanish, French, Farsi, and Greek.

Problems of Women's Liberation
Evelyn Reed

Six articles explore the social and economic roots of women's oppression from prehistoric society to modern capitalism and point the road forward to emancipation.
$15. Also in Farsi and Greek.

Puerto Rico: Independence Is a Necessity
Rafael Cancel Miranda

One of the five Puerto Rican Nationalists imprisoned by Washington for more than 25 years and released in 1979 speaks out on the brutal reality of US colonial domination, the campaign to free Puerto Rican political prisoners, the example of Cuba's socialist revolution, and the ongoing struggle for independence.
$6. Also in Spanish and Farsi.

PATHFINDER AROUND THE WORLD

Visit our website for a complete list of titles and to place orders

www.pathfinderpress.com

PATHFINDER DISTRIBUTORS

UNITED STATES
(and Caribbean, Latin America, and East Asia)

Pathfinder Books, 306 West 37th St., 13th Floor
New York, NY 10018

CANADA

Pathfinder Books, 7107 St. Denis, Suite 204
Montreal, QC H2S 2S5

UNITED KINGDOM
(and Europe, Africa, Middle East, and South Asia)

Pathfinder Books, 2nd Floor, 83 Kingsland High Street
Dalston, London, E8 2PB

AUSTRALIA
(and Southeast Asia and the Pacific)

Pathfinder, Level 1, 3/281–287 Beamish St., Campsie, NSW 2194
Postal address: P.O. Box 164, Campsie, NSW 2194

NEW ZEALAND

Pathfinder, 188a Onehunga Mall, Onehunga, Auckland 1061
Postal address: P.O. Box 3025, Auckland 1140